YOU!

What you MUST know to start your career as a professional

Howard R. Moskowitz, Ph.D.

ISBN: 143925964X
ISBN-13: 9781439259641
Library of Congress Control Number: 2009910636

DEDICATION

After a lifetime of reading, researching, writing, fighting, and occasionally winning, it's time to share some of the wisdom that has come so painfully, and yet joyfully. And with this writing comes the chance to thank three special people.

To the memory of my mother, Mrs. Leah Moskowitz, who instilled in me the discipline to continue working and writing. I did not appreciate her enough during her life. If I could wish anything for a student, I'd wish that the student could spend a year with Mom. The student would be happy, and Mom would get to shape yet another soul.

To my dear wife Arlene, who rejoices in my writing. Such joy makes writing move beyond the act of creation, beyond the expression of skill, elevating it to a spiritual dimension. Without Arlene I could not write with the soul that blesses this work. Simple as that.

And finally to my own teacher, critic, intellectual blowtorch, and late professor, S.S. (Smitty) Stevens. During the eight years that I was privileged to know him and to fear him, I could not bring myself to call him by the name everyone else called him, Smitty. I was only a student then, a frightened student, but ever so ready for education. And now, forty plus years later, it's my time to give to my students and mentorees the wisdom that Smitty gave me. Thank you, Smitty.

One final person deserves thanks. She is Michele Reisner, who, as my coauthor on books and articles, serves as one of the finest examples of one what can achieve through systematic efforts. It is such a pleasure to see her and many others at Moskowitz Jacobs, Inc., develop professionally over the years.

And so they end, the public acknowledgments and dedications. But these public words can scarce convey the real thanks that lives with me. And with these words, reader, I welcome you.

Howard R. Moskowitz, Ph. D.
White Plains, New York
September, 2009

Editing, design and layout by Linda Ettinger Lieberman and images by Paolo Gentile, Moskowitz Jacobs Inc.

TABLE OF CONTENTS

✵ ✵ ✵

CUTTING TO THE CHASE: THE BOTTOM LINE

This book describes the formative years of a research professional's development. Read it to discover what happens. Read it to learn what YOU MUST do to make this development into YOUR positive experience. The lessons contained herein will launch YOU into a positive, fulfilling, and potentially very remunerative career.

It's here. Turn the book over and over, and drain the contents dry. Absorb them. You won't be sorry.

✵ ✵ ✵

FOREWARD

The Cultures of Academe or why YOU should know what's in this book

As an introduction to this book dealing with YOU becoming a professional, I will take the liberty of presenting to you what's going on 'behind the scenes' of your education. You can fit this point of view, expose if you will, into the contents of the book you are about to read. In the next few paragraphs of this foreward we explore topics which range across science, society, education, and the marketplace.

Here, in this foreward, and writ larger in this book, is an image of the academic culture and its intellectual expressions. This image encompasses trials, tribulations, successes, and failures of our universities. I write it with optimism, hoping not to expose to the tribulation of a hemlock cocktail. So read on. It's important stuff here throughout.

Two cultures await you; choose one

To put these broad topics within a coherent context I am going to enlarge on a distinction first suggested by the British novelist, C. P. Snow. Snow divided the house of intellect into two domains, which he entitled "two cultures." Of course, these two cultures would have to be populated by different sorts of creatures; here Snow didn't let us down. The creatures were scientists and humanists. Trained as a scientist himself, the line he took in describing them was, of course, quite partisan. These lines generally are. Scientists, Snow suggested, readily understood a great deal of what the humanists were talking about. The humanists, on the other hand understood little or nothing of what the scientists were saying. Does this ring a bell? It should.

So let's visit one of Snow's novels. We find ourselves at a college function. We might hear everyone at high table laugh at a joke that referenced a quote from Hamlet or a character from Joyce. On the other hand one would expect to hear a much smaller response to a quip turning on one of Newton's Laws or some quantum mechanical gag. Not only, Snow asserted, did the humanists not understand the nature of science or the product of the scientific effort, but in their arrogance they demeaned science as mere exploitation of technology.

There was more to it, however. Snow wasn't going to let the opportunity pass without painting a picture of what was going on. Science was a grubby endeavor, not worthy to be compared either in subtlety or power to humane scholarship. In their own fields of literature and criticism, these elites believed mastery could only achieved by those with sensitivity, and the political attitudes that they mostly shared.

To the humanists, science was not a truly intellectual enterprise, and therefore scientists were not intellectuals, but rather idiot savants. It was some magic, some arcane but irrelevant knowledge which let them engage in the mechanical application of rote memory to empty mathematical formulae. The kind of arrogance Snow attributed to the humanists is vividly captured by the response of a famous professor at a major Eastern University which will here go unnamed who, when asked how many scholars he taught, replied, "*Oh, about one in a hundred.*" Feel the bite.

Miffed by the characterization of their enterprise, scientists responded to this put-down with their own Patsy. "*Of course,*" the scientists answer when the humanist attacks them as grubbers after facts, "*that is not our role.*" Indeed, their role, they argue fairly persuasively, is indistinguishable in its creative and analytical demands from the role of the scholar or critic of literature, art, and drama. "The image the humanist has in mind," the scientist responds, "*is that of the (ugh!) engineer.*" It is the engineer who panders to the demands of the populace. And through his crass exploitation of the scientists' deep knowledge, it is the engineer supplies the material delights of the public with its penchant for electric beer-can openers and synthetic eye-ball masseurs. Stung by their literary brethren, the scientists redirect that scorn for the material toward the hapless engineers trying do 'something', that is 'something useful'.

The cultures of science – what YOU face and what faces you

The two cultures are really at least three cultures. How is science 'redeemed', and indeed why does it need to be redeemed at all? The redemption of science in the eyes of the humanist is made possible by scientists themselves, who graciously, and all-too-often unknowingly kowtow to the humanities at the altar of intellectual superiority. And the sacrifice? The engineer is the hapless sacrifice, the scapegoat. This interpretation fits comfortably with the general view that engineering is somehow a less than worthy derivative of scientific knowledge. The conceit is that science formulates laws and theories, (the deep stuff), and then engineers take these laws and use them to construct dongles and doohickies.

Stop for a moment. If you think we're 'protesting too much', it's because the essence of this book is the application of science to practical problems. So it's important to put our cards right on the table. Now back to the fray.

At this point we now turn to confront the first of several cultural fairy tales which pervade popular knowledge. First is the myth of the derivative nature of practical knowledge. The legion of explainers and justifiers of science support the scientific enterprise as a fountainhead of practical consequences. Science exists to provide knowledge, and in turn to better our lives. To these explainers and justifiers, when we gain scientific knowledge we expand and extend our comprehension and control over our world. *In my opinion, this reading is (in part) the reverse of the history of science and technology. Such a view would hold that my grandmother's cooking derives from our enormous advances in organic chemistry at the turn of the present century. Fires were made and food was cooked before Lavoisier explicated the nature of combustion. Nonsense.*

Now let's turn the tables. I believe it could be argued just as persuasively that science grows with, and upon engineering advances and not vice versa. The scientific enterprise can be construed, after all, as a cleaning up operation. First, the proto-engineer succeeds in the practical mastery of some aspect of the physical, biological, or mental world. Then, and primarily then, the scientist enters (perhaps a better word is sashay in), and of course turns to an explication of the engineers successes. Although you might recoil with horror at this revision interpretation, think about it a bit as you read this foreward, and as you read the contents of this book. *By the way, this is also nonsense.*

It hardly matters which came first, because the central point that I want to make is that the function of engineering, of the PRACTICAL, is intimately connected to the function of science. Scientists can in no way disregard the work of the engineer, and my reasons for this view are not that scientific advances depend upon engineering tricks, but rather that engineering is the contract between science and humanity.

The ways in which scientific knowledge works itself through into the intellectual fabric of the common heritage involve the skills and talents of the engineer. The scientist is able to come to grips with human problems precisely because engineers have defined, explored, and operationalized the parameters within which the scientific enterprise has human consequences. Without knowledge of such consequences, pursuit of science in some purist sense serves no human purpose. If scientists are prepared to accept that their enterprise has no base in humanity, that science is an empty intellectual game, then they must also be prepared to abandon the deification of their discipline as demanding the same spiritual qualifications as the study of the humanities. The scientists must embrace the engineer as his or her contact with the human condition; if he or she rejects the engineer as a partner that defines the meaning of science in order to court the favor of the humanists, he or she abandons a humane role. In a word, practicality is spirituality. And the purist; there is room for the purist but not as the apotheosis, the epitome of what scientists should aim for.

The bottom line here is that you who read this book are entering into a new world. This is the world of applied science, engineering of the mind if you will, a world as demanding as pure science, but perhaps a great deal more fun. So read it, read as much as you wish, read the words, and read between the lines. Most of all, DO. Explore, experiment, enjoy. And in so doing you will enrich your souls, your careers, you wallets, and perhaps even yourselves.

Eugene Galanter
Emeritus Professor of Psychology &
Quondam Director of the Psychophysics Laboratory
Columbia University, New York City

BY WAY OF INTRODUCTION

It is the habit of the experienced to share what they know, or think they know, with those who are novices, just starting out in careers. The desire to share one's wisdom is not limited to the connection between professional and novice. That desire transcends such narrow boundaries, finding its expression in ethical wills by parents for their children, in books about the *rites de passage* that writers so enjoy creating, and indeed in writings about any mentor – student relation. Why should we be any different? We have as much desire to share our knowledge as the mother cow has to give milk. Take away the calf, but the desire still remains.

What is it about knowledge, about experience, about the passage through life that pushes us to share? Why do seasoned professionals suffer from this overwhelming desire to impart the secrets of success to those who, perhaps listening, are caught in a reverie of their own, in the dreams yet unfulfilled? The answer...well there is no answer, because each of us has his own reasons, coming from different backgrounds and experiences, different visions of the future.

Yet, when all is considered, hopefully you will find these words enlightening, a bit inspiring, and in some cases savvier and shrewder, albeit in a positive sense. You may well become educated about the occasional blackness of professional *realpolitik*, the yielding of idealism to practicality in the search for survival. As you read what the words, you will recognize some of your own experiences, perhaps a bit edited, farcified, but your own experiences nevertheless. Enjoy what you read, and when you come upon yourself, stop for a minute and enjoy the rest of the ride with eyes opened up even wider.

☆ ☆ ☆

PART I

GETTING EDUCATED

CHAPTER 1

THE VALUE OF KNOWLEDGE:
WHAT YOU SHOULD LEARN, AND WHY

Introduction

College and graduate school provide wonderful opportunities to get trained in a field. Today you will encounter dozens, perhaps even hundreds of people who are experts in specific subjects. Their resumes are festooned with their specialization in a minute area, in their accomplishments in that area. Garlands of accomplishments drop from the edge of each page, experience, insight, wisdom. The sense from reading these resumes is that the person is an expert, even at the age of 25 or so.

It ain't necessarily so, however. A lot of what you see in resumes is the consequence of training in a specific area, in the ability to do some particular activity well, and the ability to carry out investigations in a tiny, probably irrelevant topic. You may not see evidence of education. And it is to education that we turn first. Education is the foundation of everything. Without it, you might just as well be a quick typist with access to Google®.

What should you learn in college?

College typically represents the first opportunity to get some serious education. There are instances when an individual begins true education in high school, but for the most part one is simply too young. The critical faculties are not yet formed, so even though the person might wish to become educated at the younger age, more than likely the maturity is years away, and what one learns are facts, not truths. There's nothing wrong with the person wanting to be educated and failing to be educated in high school. The mind is not yet ready, not sufficiently seasoned, and not able to appreciate what the person reads, sees, and hears. It's just a matter of readiness.

The value of a liberal education

A recurring theme in this book is the need for education, rather than for training. But what type of education? Many young professionals feel that it's a waste of time to get a classical education, filled or perhaps bejeweled with history, languages, literature. Some even feel that mathematics and science may be too hard, and that it's probably better to get an education in business. One of the most common questions from young students just graduating and beginning their careers in business/science (i.e., product development or market research) is about the value of an MBA. Their question is really about the value of their education, and the possible nirvana that will be theirs if they could only get the magic MBA degree.

So what are we to tell these students and earnest enquirers? What is the real value of liberal education? Is it worth pursuing in these beginning decades of the 21st century, or ought we to relegate the previously hallowed liberal education to the dustbin of history, as something that worked, but in the olden days? Is it sufficient today merely to be facile in finding information rather than absorbing, digesting, and incorporating such information into one's own being?

The reality is that the value of a liberal education is to be found in the second word, education. We don't mean training here, and we don't mean becoming conversant with the newest business practices, the newest science fads, and the latest and greatest in computer technology. We mean by a liberal education the intercourse with the great minds, through reading, thinking, challenging. And we mean the great questions, not the particular minutiae of science and business practice. Aristotle, Aquinas, Dante, Michelangelo, and hundreds, thousands of writers, coped with problems of life, of experience, of art. The student would be best advised to revel in their work, swim in the current of thought, the ocean of ideas. There's time enough later on to specialize, to read the works that will be forgotten in days. A liberal education is the bedrock of a lifetime. This type of foundation is worth spending time creating, laying down, and making sure it's rock solid. A liberal education is truly the basis of future achievements.

What history teaches you

We could talk all day about a liberal education. It's in the specifics, however, that we go somewhere. Otherwise, we're likely to spout platitudes, such as a liberal education makes a person a better citizen. It may or may not, but we have no idea of what a liberal education is from that hogwash, nor do we know what a better citizen is, or perhaps don't even care.

So let's go into the specifics. Those of you reading these words are most likely hopeful, budding young professionals, or perhaps even 're-naiscing' old professionals on a soul-searching expedition to the next stage. So, it's likely that you've come in contact with history somewhere during your education. It's not likely that you've been exposed to the intellectual history of your own field – we're all too much in a hurry to bother with what's passed. We're really more interested in the future.

With this bit of long winded introduction what then do we learn from history? Is history simply, as Henry Ford is reputed to have said, one damn thing after another? Or does history have a grand purpose, a magnificent story to tell us? And, of course, if we are scientists, then what do we learn from history that make us better in our jobs, careers, profession?

We begin with the truism, or perhaps just plain factoid that history is not simply a collection of facts. Anyone can compile facts. Go to the library, get out books of history, and compile your own. If you are the one of the specialty sciences, it may be a bit harder. The source material isn't commonly available as it is for world history (especially European history). You'll have to go to the library, do some digging, try to determine what's happening, look for patterns, and so forth. And most important, tell a story which interests someone besides yourself.

So for the budding young scientist, just of what use is history? Well, for one, science does not operate in a vacuum. Just because you, the reader, may be entering the profession full of 'new ideas' and in the words of many 'full of piss and vinegar' doesn't mean that you are entering uncharted waters. Most likely now, at the start or early part of your career you're traveling on well trodden paths. And, even many of the new discoveries that you have made or about to make are some modest departures from what is known. Of course, later on as your career progresses you may find yourself in these waters, in worlds unknown. But even then, you'll find a history of your field to help you in these uncharted waters. They may not be so new after all.

And so the role of history here? Well, a good sense of history, first of general world history, then of some specific area, and finally history of your own scientific field, pays off. History gives you a sense of who and what you are, of the importance of the human being in the unfolding story of the world, of the numerous detail which goes into the story of human efforts. Take these lessons and apply them to your own field. Don't assume just because you have been well educated in a method, a technique, a series of data-gathering maneuvers, that you really are knowledgeable about your field.

Furthermore, just knowing today's literature of your field doesn't make you a scientist. It makes you well read today, but not knowledgeable.

A good exercise in your field is to trace the intellectual development backwards, from where you are to a generation back, and then a generation before that, and so forth. But don't stop there. Don't just trace the history. Ask the question 'why'. What happened to make a researcher think a certain way?

For example, in the world of consumer testing of products a lot of practitioners have espoused methods such as 'mapping', where they locate the products on a geometrical map. Management in R&D and marketing accept mapping methods to the point where marketing journals feature articles with these maps. We're talking now of a history that goes back 30-40 years.

> *With that history, the real question is 'why'. And the 'why' is not simple. We're not talking about 'what', about the best methods for mapping the stimulus, about the so-called 'latest and greatest' featured by one or another practitioner, in an attempt to secure professional position and advantage. We're talking about a far more profound question — why did practitioners adopt the*

mapping method? What was so attractive? What did the practitioner learn? And, how has this type of thinking affected the development of knowledge on the one hand and business practice on the other. It is these types of questions about 'history' that are important. And, such questions invite the young scientist to so his homework, and by doing so become a better professional, more knowledgeable, more informed, more aware.

Felicitous language – the use of literature

We're surrounded by literature. Just go into any airport bookstore and scan the books. A lot of the books are today's current best sellers. These are books. They're not literature, except by a stretch.

Literature is hard to define, but like pornography it exists and there is some intuitive standard so you can sense what it is when you see it. Perhaps a good rule to follow is go after the 'great books'. The great books aren't named so because they're potboilers. Rather, they deal with enduring topics, with the struggles of people, with situations, with hopes, fears, emotions, and the complexities of life. And they deal with ideas, some with the ideas percolating to the surface, others with the ideas embedded deeply within the story, the description, the evolution of the personas of the people in the book.

And so, you might ask, why bother? The answer is the famous five letter radio station: WiiFM (what's in it for me?). The simple answer is that you become better from reading literature. Except that that's not the real truth. The more appropriate answer is that literature gives you a sense of other lives, other values. You, and in fact all of us, live within the confine of your own constricted life, paying attention to your own problems, dealing with the most important being in the world, YOU (or speaking from the first person singular, ME, I, MINE, MY and the host of other ways of focusing on that most important of all people). Literature pulls you out of your own world, inviting you to visit other worlds, inhabited by other creatures, like you, but with other problems, other ways of dealing with issues. In a sense literature is the world where you, and everyone really, are not, but should be. Through literature we all grow, because we see laid out in front of us other parallel lives.

But, you ask, why is literature so important for us? Well, the answer is that without literature we end up narrowing our already-narrow little world into even more constricted knots. It's not the habit of young researchers to be young poets, artists, sensitive individuals, although the occasional individual may be all of the above. Most of the time the young researcher is busy chasing chimeras, respect of colleagues, grants, publications, with scarcely a moment even to accept the existence of other people, much less understand these people. And so it is left to literature to force the eye to other worlds, and the soul to share in experiences that might otherwise be entirely overlooked in the attempt to become the scientist, and the forgetting of what it is like to become a person.

If the foregoing isn't enough, then there is one more reason to study literature. The reason is that there are an awful lot of good writers in world literature. It helps to read them, to get a sense of how other people craft sentences.

> *When you read the scientific literature (and that includes business research) you will find it to be the antithesis of good literature. For the most part the sentence constructions are tortuous, if they can be even at all discerned. Moving further, you will find that the scientific literature is not a pleasure to read. Very few people would read what scientists write to get a sense of what happens in the laboratory, to feel the excitement of science, to get a whiff of discovery. Instead the writing is constricted, almost to the point where the density outweighs the information. Scientific literature is hard to follow, even when you know the topic intimately. It's good to read real literature, by real writers, about real life, to get a sense of what you could accomplish when you report the results of your efforts.*

<u>Walking through libraries</u>

One of my most wonderful memories takes place in the Harvard psychology library on the 6th floor of William James Hall in Cambridge. It was the policy of the graduate school to allow its graduate students unlimited access to the specialty libraries. Graduate students were considered professionals in training. And, of course, there was the point of view of i.e. Boring, *eminence gris* of Harvard's psychology, to wit *'anyone who knows the difference between work and play doesn't belong here'*.

And so the psychology library, a modest room filled at that time with archival journals and books on experimental psychology. Tracing its heritage to the late 19th Century and to its break with philosophy, the psychology library presented in its collection and arrangement a one-of-a-kind yet tantalizingly available history of experimental psychology. Side by side were journals that contained historical papers along with lots of other papers that by today's standards are too long, not readable. Or in other words, G-d awful stuff.

But what about this library? It's not the journals, not the books, not even the free access to the stacks that we graduates had. Rather, was a sense of belonging to a tradition. We were free to wander the library at any time, to touch, to look, to read old journals jammed side by side with the newest numbers of other learned journals. The experience was heady. Of course a bit daunting at first, but the sheer immanence of the library, its ready, welcoming at any time with the merest turn of the key issued to us sufficed to make a magic experience.

What about the relevance of this library to the new professional? Today's libraries are locked in mortal combat with knowledge from search. With Google®, scanned papers in JSTOR®, and with the ready availability of knowledge at a single click there's the very real possibility that such wonderful experiences as walking the stacks will become a memory of the past, or even worse, an underappreciated ritual that the new student endures, much as one has to endure other meaningless activities because they hearken back to some wonderful past.

To use a metaphor of today, walking through a library is accessing information in a linear way. You actually have to look at the books, have to see other information. Just the act of walking through the library forces you to take in other impressions, other ideas. You may not be particularly cognizant, aware, even conscious of what you're seeing, but the sum of the visual impressions make the difference. Long after you have found the information you're looking for in a journal, tucked away in some stack, amidst dozens of other bound volumes, you'll remember the other articles in that journal. You may not care, and in fact, for most of the articles it's hard to care. But you will get a sense of the article as a small, but integral, part of a bigger whole of knowledge.

Let's finish our walk through the library by comparing that to the way today's researchers all too often find information (the writer included!). Well, we know the topic that we are researching; that's the good thing. We don't need to go to a library; that's maybe good, maybe not so good. We sit in front of the computer, log on to Google or some other search engine, and even Google Scholar®, type in the information. We may be specific in our search in which case we get a few to a few dozen hits. Or we may be more general in our search, and get hundreds, perhaps thousands. Google Scholar® will return to us a lot of other valuable information, such as others who cite the article, and so forth.

Our computer-based search is effective, efficient, and does the job in a way that we could not have done before. But what are we missing? The smell of the old? Do we get that same sense of excitement, of belonging to a field, of holding and touching the work of others? Do we experience that rush of insight that links together disparate articles in one journal number? Do we get a sense of history, of what we are doing framed against a larger background? Hardly; we do get what we need, but we don't get the experience. We get the product, but not necessary the part of the education that we didn't even realize was there to be gotten.

Why mathematics?

Mathematics, the queen of the sciences, should be on everyone's curriculum. It is nothing short of criminal for colleges to let the student skip mathematics when the student has declared a major in humanities. Of course, you will ask again why? It's a fair question. After all, mathematics is not like a survey course in history or American /

European / Asian culture, or a survey course in art. Mathematics is hard work. There's nothing trivial about working through a proof of a theorem, of understanding why a proof 'must proceed' a certain way, It darned hard work.

But, the work is worth it. Of course we all know that it will be a rare day when you will use the mathematical proofs over which you labor so hard. Yet, the effort can't help but inform your thinking, force you to confront what you know and what you don't know. You see, when you study mathematics, you either understand it or you don't understand it. You can't fool yourself. You may be able to *pffmpf* your way through an explanation, but the truth of the matter is that you yourself know whether you 'see it', and understand, or whether you're going through the motions. And that honesty is important.

And while we're talking about knowledge and mathematics, let's get it over with -- Statistics, sadistics, and statics

Mention the word mathematics and a goodly number of people will wince. Mention the word statistics and you won't get a wince, but you're likely to get story after story. What is it about the measurement and mathematics of events, their frequency and plausibility that takes statistics out of the realm of agony and makes it into the substance of stories recounted with the greatest relish, with a smile showing through the groans? Hearing stories about statistics is somewhat like hearing about the person's recent operation, the drugs that the person has to take on a regular basis, symptoms, and the like. Full of life, sometimes too full.

First, let's talk about statistics in the way students learn it. We aren't talking here about mathematics, about the foundations of statistics. Rather, we are talking about its applications, about putting numbers to events, and making some conclusions about those numbers. Some of our conclusions will invoke the notion of random error. Other conclusions deal with patterns in the data, relations among variables, and what might these relations inform us about the world.

> As you well know, statistics divides into two different parts, inferential and pattern fitting. Inferential statistics are well known to most students, indeed all-too-well. Inferential statistics deal the odds that a specific observation one makes comes from random variation or comes from a 'true effect'. Of course, ask most people, even graduate students in the throes of their training, about what these statistics mean and you're not likely to get more than the foregoing answer. To the vast majority of scientists, statistics is a finishing coat of paint they put to their observations; sort of like sealer to the data.
>
> Let's look into each of the aforementioned topics – type of statistics, response to statistics, and response to statisticians. We might seem to belabor the point, but

its worth noting that most scientists work with statistics, work with statisticians, and have at one or another time endured recriminations and hostile reviews based on the statistics in a paper that they may have submitted for publication. So a somewhat longer digression on statistics is probably worth the effort.

Of course each researcher carries around particular biases about statistics. Whether or not we are conversant with the methods, feel comfortable or downright fearful, we carry with us biases about what types of statistics are 'right', what types are simply 'frightening', and what statistics are actually helpful. We also carry around with us an almost instinctive reaction to statisticians, those who practice the often arcane art of statistical analysis. We respond to these individuals in a way that we probably don't respond to anyone else in our lives – a combination of respect, fear, and acute intellectual discomfort. Sort of like responding to a shaman, albeit a research shaman.

We began this section with the statement that statistics divides into two main areas – inferential statistics on the one hand and modeling (or data mining, or other au courant phrase) on the other. And herein lies some of the problem that you face as a professional. It's one thing to make an observation about nature. You can be careful, you can be an exquisite observer, meticulously detailed, agonizingly exact. (There are a lot of people like that). Then, after you have made the observations it's time to do the 'quant work'. What do we mean by this term 'quant work?' Quite simply it's the rigorous analysis of the data, outside of your hands, done according to specific rules, using numbers to let you make statements about what you have discovered!

Inferential statistics: This is what most people think about when they mention the word statistics. The notion here is a bit unnerving; that the measurements you so carefully made may or may not be statistically significant. But what is this idea of significance really all about? A lot of people incorrectly believe that something that is statistically significant is relevant. That's not the true meaning of 'significant'. Rather, significant means that if you were to repeat this study 100 times, the average result would not be 0, at least 95% of the time. This is hardly a vote of confidence for the relevance of your research efforts. Nor should it be. Inferential statistics simply deal with the probability that the mean you are observing is not 0, or is not another pre-defined value.

There's really very little zip and romance when it comes to inferential statistics. It the main, inferential statistics is cookbook statistics. You learn it like you learn any other hygiene practice; what to do, how to report it. And, when it comes time to report your results in the scientific literature (i.e., when you submit a paper), you want to be blessed by the statistician that your results are significant. It's not what the data mean that is important. It's rather '*did you do the appropriate hygiene on your data, and have it ritually blessed according to the rules of inferential statistics?*' It should not come as a surprise that people are both frightened of inferential statistics, and very obedient to the commands of the statistician, because in this case the statistician's job is to bless the data.

Data mining and pattern discovery: As unpleasant as inferential statistics might be (sort of like your flu shot or your colonoscopy), there's another area of statistics that can be joyfyl. This is data mining, pattern discovery, exploratory data analysis, or any of another half dozen names.

During the past two decades, and with the help of the personal computer, a new discipline in statistics has emerged. The objective of this other area of statistics is to discover patterns in the data. Notice that the word patterns is used, not the word significance. Data miners or exploratory analysts look for patterns, for what might be happening, for hints about the person as revealed in the mass of data. There may be hypothesis, guesses about what might be going on, but rarely specific tests that come out significant or insignificant. Looking for patterns doesn't demand adherence to significance and approved ways of testing. Looking for patterns demands, well, looking for regularities that might be hints of deeper things going on. This can be a lot of fun. And, it's here, in the search for patterns, where mathematics and statistics come alive, where the investment of learning is worthwhile for your professional development.

So, what's the bottom line here? What are we to make of statistics? Since we're talking about education and formation, rather than about substantive, there are four considerations things of import to YOU before you give into your rash step to drop statistics, and remain blissfully inumerate:

1. If you stop at inferential statistics, then for the most part your use of statistics will be uninspired. That is, you will end up using statistics to assure your audience and perhaps yourself that the results you report are not really 'random'. And then what?

2. If you stop at inferential statistics, more than likely your focus on statistics will be one of nervous self-doubt! Yes, that's worth repeating. Nervous self-doubt! You won't be asking yourself what you have learned, but rather is what you're doing statistically significant. You will always be asking yourself whether you are doing the 'right test'. You won't learn, but rather you will use the test as a 'check off', something that you did because 'it's required'.

3. You won't have the joy of moving on with any sort of real ability to data mining, where nature may reveal herself to you in more accommodating ways. Stay with your statistics, and you'll be able to discover more. A lot more.

4. The statisticians who you will meet in these two aspects of statistics will differ a great deal from each other. There will be some who love the hygiene, who can help you do the best possible test. And there will be others who will love to help you with the data, those who enjoy mucking around in the results, looking for patterns. Enjoy working with both, but recognizing that they are radically different individuals, with different ways of looking at the world, and with different souls. It's likely that you will resonate with one type more than with another. Which one will make you feel comfortable is an empirical question, to be answered when you do your next experiment.

✡ ✡ ✡

CHAPTER 2

THE LURE OF INDUSTRY AND THE CROWN OF ACADEME: SELLING YOUR SOUL OR JUST RENTING IT?

<u>Introduction</u>

It should not come as a surprise that most new researchers, especially those with Ph.D.s, find themselves caught between a rock and a hard place, between the Scylla of science and the Charybdis of paying rent.

For those of you who don't know what a rock and a hard place, its colloquial for the horns of a dilemma, neither choice is good.

For those of you who don't know what Scylla and Charybydis, here is the more eloquent Wikipedia® definition:

> *The phrase between Scylla and Charybdis, although infrequently used today, has meant having to choose between two unattractive choices, and is the progenitor of the phrase "<u>between a rock and a hard place</u>."…..*

> *The Romantic poet Percy Bysshe Shelley used Scylla and Charybdis in an analogy of how society is poised between anarchy and despotism in his work, in defense of poetry. The passage reads:*

> *'The rich have become richer, and the poor have become poorer; and the vessel of the state is driven between the Scylla and Charybdis of anarchy and despotism'*

Whether we use today's colloquial phrase or yesterday's mythology, the choice of what to do after the degree remains a tough one. Do you sell out, as you will be accused by others who choose to pursue science for its own sake? Or do you remain noble, impoverished for the sake of science, for that noble cause which spurred your study?

Well, the truth is that the question is nonsense. When anyone asks you that question, or even when anyone even begins to hint that you're selling out because you're getting a job in industry rather than in academia, you can be assured that you're dealing with a jealous phony. Perhaps 40 years ago or so, when the author received his Ph.D., there might have been this issue of 'selling out', but no longer. It's perfectly respectable to have a real job after the Ph.D., rather than becoming a post doc, and perhaps after that a lowly paid instructor. Not that the academic life is to be sneered at, but rather the business life has its own attractions.

The why

It's not which you choose, academia or industry, but rather why others are so damned concerned. What is the reason for people to look askance at someone going into industry? Is it because that person is somehow abandoning a holy cause, giving up vows, exchanging the world of holiness for the world of the secular, perhaps even profane? Is the person choosing the world of applied research, or even management any less of a professional than the person who nobly follows a career of basic research to further the compass of science?

Perhaps some of the reason underlying this notion of 'selling out' is the need for the individual pursuing a scientific career to justify his or her own actions. In fact, years of experience in life will teach that many acts of a person are done in order to protect one's own image of oneself, one's *amour propre*. Protesting that another person will simply 'disappear' when the latter person fails to pursue a pure scientific career says much about the needs of the person doing the saying, rather than about the person receiving the advice. So the practical strategy to deal with the issue of 'choice' is to ask 'why'. What's the reason for the question in the first place? And, always remember: Just the fact that the individual is responding so strongly to your desire for commercial success should tip you off.

Having it both ways – industry and science

You don't need to sacrifice the academic world in order to enjoy the fruits of the business world, the excitement of a life in commerce. Over the past several decades enlightened management in all types of companies have come to realize that many of their professionals want to have some of their cake and eat it, want to do applied work, but at the same time want to publish and maintain a professional reputation. For the most part companies realize that to keep their staff happy, especially those with these desires to merge business and academic activities they must allow their employees who are professionals to pursue professional goals, not just business ones.

If you are truly interested in blending the scientific and business careers, no doubt you're going to go into one of the staff service jobs in a company. You won't go into marketing or general management for a very simple reason. There won't be any time, or much of an opportunity to publish there, or to meet scientific colleagues. The people you will meet when you go into marketing will be marketers, perhaps trained at business schools in research methods (your interest), but not particularly motivated or even able to practice it. So it's more likely you'll be in the technical area, not the business area.

> *Get used to it. That's the way the world is. You can have what you want…*
> *but you better be ready to give up the dream of getting to the top. Unless, of*
> *course, you or your parents own the company. But that's not relevant here.*

Creating a scientific career within the company

How do you go about following your interest in science in a company, without getting swallowed up? One thing is certain when you work for a company that you do not own. Your interest in science is not the company's interest, no matter what you might think after the interview. The business of the company is profit, growth, and any of the hundred different objectives that businesses have. But these are not the business of science.

Do not for a moment be fooled by the sweet talk, by the posters on the wall, by the publicity that the company sends out about its interest in science. Certainly there may be some truth to what you hear, what you read. But, you are interested in the most important person in your life, YOU. The company is interested in the most important organization in its life, the COMPANY. And, YOU are not the COMPANY. Nor is the COMPANY YOU. That's all there is.

That being said, the reality OF the company does not necessarily destroy your opportunity WITH the company. Rather, we just demarcated the boundary between you and the company. When you take the job, for whom will you work?

You have a limited number of hours in your lifetime. Treat them as precious; they are. When you begin your career you think you will live forever. That misconception and hubris, that miscalculation of your position in the universe, is the privilege of the young. But don't let that miscalculation lead you astray, indulging yourself in the fantasy that 'some day, but not now, I will follow MY dreams of scientific achievement'. When you start your career you begin at the bottom. At the bottom is where you take orders. *And, generally, not from someone interested in your career. That is, the start of your career just isn't about you.*

First steps – sniff out the opportunity

When you get to the company stop for a little while to get a sense, an intuitive feel of the culture that you sense, or just 'get'. What's happening? What is going on here? It is this intangible web of relations, goals, activities, this thing called culture, which will help or hinder you in your efforts to create YOUR professional reputation.

Look around for a little bit, preferably before you join the company, saying a happy yes to that offer. Who works there? Not their titles, but they themselves. What is their nature? What do they talk about? Or do they even talk about what they do? Do you sense joy or drudgery? Have people been there for years, or do they come and go, like a revolving door? Do people who have been at the company a long time have 'standing' in the outside world? Or are they little corporate beings, 'Ned Dweebs', nobodies, with a bit of power? It is a culture of KNOW? Or a culture of NO? This is not meant as a pun, but a deadly serious question.

Now, for some other things of more specific and relevant natures. Does the company actively suppress individual creativity? If so, this is important to find out early in the game. Your entire career may depend on knowing it, and accepting the terms that such corporate culture dictates.

> *Years ago, in the 1970's and 1980's companies like Procter & Gamble would actively suppress the individual. That's not to say that all individuals were suppressed, but rather that P&G tried to impress on all its corporate employees the need for secrecy, for maintaining a low profile, for interacting with the professional public in a way that allowed no one any insight into the P&G workings. The approach was exceptionally successful. P&G employees traveled in groups, did not share knowledge, and took in rather than shared. In the end, P&G won a great deal, but the individual employees ended up as professional ciphers, for the most part. Of course, after someone retired from P&G it was quite possible to make a living for a few years going to companies and telling everyone about the P&G way. Those uptight days are long past now, but they may be very much part of the 'today' of other companies.*

You can find out a lot about a company by talking to its employees, preferably the approachable younger and middle level employees. The older, lifer-employees and those in top management have already absorbed the corporate culture. These acculturated individuals may not realize that the company is excessively conscious about security, and suppresses the growth of its employees. You're more likely to get an honest story by talking to the young people, still full of dreams. How are they making their dreams happen? How exactly? What is the corporation doing? Search for more than platitudes. Search for actual behaviors that you can point to.

<u>Okay – you accepted the job, you got oriented, you have your cubicle, now what?</u>

Having explored the opportunity in your company, what next do you do? The answer isn't simply do what you want to advance your scientific interests. Undoubtedly when you are entering a company you are entering a minefield. It's good to know where the traps are, and where the safe zones lie. The same holds true for the university, but in fact that university's games and minefields are far more subtle, requiring an entire encyclopedia of advice. Companies are a lot easier because the ostensible purpose of the company is to make money. That purpose isn't necessarily the purpose of the individual employees, each of whom comes equipped with an individualized set of desires, stratagems, good points, and insufferable bad ones. However, one can always appeal to the profit motive as a general goal. It works.

Now back to the company.

Rule #1 – you're always better asking forgiveness than permission. When you are given your chance or you grab a chance to do some research and advance your career, it's better to do it and then spend time explaining what you did than to forego this opportunity because you might not receive everyone's blessing. (You can also read the previous sentence more bluntly as....you might piss off someone). It's always better to have something of your own achievement in your back pocket, done, ready to be shown to others, putting you in the more active position, than having to rely impotently on the kindness of others. And, going one step further, having your own research results gives you some currency with which to bargain. Having no research results means perhaps that you haven't irritated someone in the short run, but that you've short-changed yourself in the long run.

Rule #2 – go for the early, fast and easy hits, rather than going for something that is long term. In the long run we're all dead. And, in a corporation you may be dead a lot faster than you think. With this in mind, it's better to go out with stuff in your pocket to show to the outside world. Small, simple experiments will serve you better than longer term ones. It's just a matter of the way the world works. Your next employer will be more interested in what you accomplished, the experiments you ran, the findings you made, rather than in your grand dreams. You and your mother may live on dreams; your employer and future employer do not. Aim for stuff, to have and to hold, not perhaps never-to-be-achieved dreams in a tomorrow that may not come. Remember the old adage – a bird in the hand is worth two in the bush (or two in the design phase!). So, better flame out than rust out.

Rule #3 – simple is better. We'll deal with the 'art' of giving a company presentation later on. The key point made here is that you want to be as simple as possible when talking about what you have done, and what you see for the future. When you start your career by presenting results, make sure that you have simple-to-understand findings. Simple is not only good, it's really the only thing. There's a reason for this. You are trying to establish your reputation. You're likely not to know as much as the other people in the room. So, be simple and clear. You're just starting. You should be modest. You don't have much else, *YET*. With a few results you can present a reasonably tasty dish. It's sort of like onions and fat. You start a lot of good cooking with that. It's simple, clear, to the point.

Rule #4 – Learn to shut up. As you create your own world in a company, recognize that you are in the presence of other individuals with similar needs. People are insecure, nervous, worried about how they appear. Give the other people a chance to talk about their vision. It's not about you. It's about YOUR FUTURE. And, to some degree it's about how you share your future with others, to make them part of your team.

This isn't psycho-babble. We're not talking about *'I'm okay..you're ok'*, or any of that stuff. We're talking about making room in your future for other people. Keep quiet after you begin talking, and see how quickly the others rush in to help you. Remember that…and remember that the sound of a person's voice is the sweetest melody for that person.

A time to hold (your cards) and a time to fold (your cards) – know when to move on

Ok, so you've begun your career in the company. You've done everything more or less right. The truth of the matter is that you've screwed up a couple of things, but people don't remember because for the most part people don't really care. But not you're getting long of tooth. Perhaps you've been at the company for a few years. You look around, and you feel your scientific growth isn't going anywhere. Now what?

There's no simple answer to holding or folding, staying or leaving. The first thing you should keep in mind is don't leave without a place to go. The second thing is don't leave unless the place you're going to is where you want to stay for a while. Life has a strange way of depositing us in deserts, or stranding us on far away islands, and a variety of places where we are going to be just plain unhappy And, the story about people you know who somehow find 'wonderful jobs' after leaving your company may just be that – stories, wish fulfillment. The grass may be greener somewhere else … or it just may be painted hay, that's all.

On the other hand, sometimes you just have to leave. Some companies are toxic. Some companies may never give you a chance to create your own scientific career. Oh, certainly these companies will have wonderful signs on the wall, to the effect that their employees are the most important resource they have, or ideas are critical, or some other nonsense that companies pay other professionals good money to create, spew out, and tack up on the wall. *'Pour encourager les autres'*. If, in your heart of hearts, you realize that there is no future, that the corporate blather is simply that, politically correct nonsense, and if you feel that you have to go, then go. It's better to be outside of a toxic world than inside. Of course, if you want to go very much but the world inside is not toxic, then we're back to square one – stay or leave. It's a hard question.

So what's the bottom line here? What's the wisdom you ought to absorb? Well, first, don't rush. Look around. Keep your mouth shut and absorb. That's why you have two ears and one mouth, rather than the other way around.

Second, look around again. Is it better outside? Really better? Can you point to specifics, to identifiable opportunities that YOU can get? If you can, then go after them. If you can't, then hang tight. It can always get worse where you are, and when it gets too bad you can reconsider leaving.

Finally, look at people who worked in the company before you. Did they achieve more in their scientific career when they left? Really? We're not talking about what they say, but what they do, and who they are. Try writing their 'obituary'. What do you have to say about them in their latest job? Remember, you're memorializing them. There must be something very good about them in their last job.

Above all, shut up. The Ethics of the Fathers, the wisdom tractate in the Mishna, tells us that silence is the 'fence for wisdom'.

Deeper thoughts – selling out?

Up to now in this chapter we have talked about what to do, in an operational sense, to get an idea of whether the company you joined will allow you to create your scientific career. However, the notion of selling your soul or renting it goes far beyond this Machiavellian-inspired issue of opportunity. When it comes to working for a company, there is a much more profound set of feelings and considerations. We now deal with them.

Let's begin by looking at the newly minted professional. The phrase 'newly-minted' itself is worth dissecting for a moment, because language has a wonderful way of capturing the truth in a succinct, economical way. We talk about newly-minted coins, about coins that have just been created by the machinery of the treasury. Newly-minted means pristine, shiny, not yet filled with experienced. Newly-minted means no individuation yet. All these coins look alike. And newly-minted excites within paints the word picture of a university system that stamps out these humans in a cold, automatic sort of a way, like the machine stamps out the coin. Wonderful picture, great metaphor.

When you emerge from your training (you never emerge from education) typically a Ph.D., but also a master's degree, people will tell you in uncountable platitudes that the world is open to you.

Now is the moment, after the degree, when you begin to think about what you should do. Academic education for the most part extols the creation of knowledge, the human effort to understand the world, the importance of publishing your findings. And, for many years, academics held themselves to be a higher form of being, not 'polluted' by the crass commercialism of industry, but rather free to pursue noble goals, knowledge and wisdom. Of course in the reality of everyday life the academic world is just as filled as are companies with crassness, backbiting and all the wonderful things which gleefully and deliciously destroy our moral character. However, in the fantasy of the academics, the life of the mind itself, with the particulars conveniently ignored, is held up as the noble idea, the *summum bonum*, pearl without price, for the newly-minted professional.

And this vision of your future is what you have to decide about. Are you going to follow the academic dream, enjoy a life of the mind, publications beyond count, achievements in the realm of knowledge? Or are you going to follow another dream, a different star, and make your way in a company, perhaps compromising your dreams? Just know one thing. In the end we all compromise, academic and business person, scholar and administrator alike. It's not the general path you will take, but the particulars with which YOU feel comfortable. You are not selling out, not really, when you leave academics for industry and commerce. You're simply choosing another world in which to compromise.

There are three paths – which one leads where you want to go?
The truth of the matter is that no author's words can really help you make up your mind. The reality in which you find yourself defies any author 'feel-goods', any vacuous psycho-babble that tells you the decision is up to you. You must really understand yourself first. Try talking to yourself and answering honestly.

The reality of the situation is both far easier and far harder than alluded to here. First, the easy part. The decisions that you make at the very earliest part of your career (1-3 years after the degree) don't really matter in terms of what you write, what you produce. You'll have a chance to do really great work later on. Second, the hard part. The decisions that you make at the very earliest part of your career could matter a great deal, not in substance, but in the choices that will become available. Your decisions will affect the opportunity to make choices later on. These decisions may open up new doors, or close them.

With the gravity and the irrelevance of your actions both in mind, and yes, dealing with the contradiction in your head, let's look at three paths you might take.

Path #1…research is in your heart and mind: When you choose to work for a company, you may not be allowed to do research. If you have research in your heart, if you are filled with the desire to do research, then it's likely that you and the said company will part ways.

Path #2…you can take research..or leave it: It's just your day job: On the other hand, if the company prevents you from doing research, and the truth is that you don't like research all that much, there's won't be much of a burning desire to leave for another 'research position'. Why? It should be obvious; you're not going to where there is promise of fulfilling your life's ambition. You really don't care as much about research. So, there's no real reason to leave. And … the rest of the story? You'll stay there, until something better comes your way.

Path #3…you choose science a post-doctoral fellowship … but with the WRONG scientist. After finishing a Ph.D. many young researchers feel it is necessary to broaden one's horizon, and necessary to establish one's own identity. You can't really do that in the laboratory where you studied, unless all the stars are in alignment. So, you look around, ask about scientists and institutions accepting postdoctoral fellows. You find one, and a researcher who seems, by all signs, to be competent. Yet, you find out later on that your post-doc is with someone who the field does not respect. What a nightmare. Here you are at a disadvantage; no reputation, dependent entirely upon what you realize may well turn out to be a 'non-starter'. You may end up losing years by this wrong decision..or...you may end up not suffering at all. By all means, when you discover the fit is wrong..then go.

Summing up

The moral of the story is to do what you feel is best for right now. But, at the same time, keep thinking about what you want to do in two years, in five years, and in ten years. And, as you project yourself into the future, you may sense a discomfort, a dis-ease about what you are doing now. Pay attention to that quiet, soft voice in the middle of your head, that nagging feeling. When it comes, there's a message. It's your intuition and your soul talking to you. Listen.

✻ ✻ ✻

CHAPTER 3

THE DANCE OF MENTORING

Introduction

Not all relations between teachers and students are formal, embedded in a particular educational system, with the promise of a degree at the end of the tunnel. Sometimes a student looks for a certain person to become a teacher; the teacher may not even have a formal academic position in the school. Such a student-teacher relation is the essence of mentoring. The relation is not formal, there are no specific demands of performance, there are no grades to be given, and there is no set time for the relation to begin or to end.

Mentoring is an important part of an education, despite the reality that it is informal, often unrecognized, all too frequently unappreciated. Indeed, many students learn more from being mentored by professionals with experience than they may learn in their formal classes, chock-filled as those are with reading assignments, papers to be written and exams.

The secret to mentoring is that the interchange between mentor and mentored deals with aspects that are important to the latter's professional life, at the time that these aspects are taking on reality which they did not have before. And, if truth be told, the mentor may get as much out of the relation as does the mentored. That 'something' is a renewed sense of purpose, and the freshness of spirit which can come only from those starting the journey, filled with hope, not cynicism.

Mentoring versus advising

It's common today to hear the word mentor used, sometimes in school, but far more often in one's early career. It's also common to hear the word adviser. Both are figures of importance for the student and the young professional. These are not the same, however, and even the feelings of the words differ.

The word *adviser* has a formal tone, a sense of giving advice, of giving knowledge in a structured way. When we use the word adviser, such as in the business-jargon of 'trusted adviser' to name one example, we have a sense of the Italian *consigliore*, the adviser to the prince, the wise person who gives suggestions. In high school and in college we also use the word adviser in much the same way. The adviser stands back, assays the situations, and suggests. There is a sense of an invisible wall between the adviser and the person being advised, with that wall being impossible to scale. The adviser possesses some knowledge, and in the formal capacity, gives that knowledge over to the person whom is being advised. And finally, there is no sense of the two people sharing anything but the guidance, no emotion, no bonding. The adviser suggests, the advisee may or may not follow the suggestion. In essence then, there is no journey together, just the handing over of a point of view from a person wiser in this aspect to a person seeking that wisdom.

☆ ☆ ☆

Now turn to your reactions to the word 'mentor'. Compare the word 'mentor' side by side with the word 'adviser'. There's an emotional side to 'mentor', a feeling of closeness, a feeling of sharing something spiritual. Mentor conjures up the bond of connection, closeness, the feeling of the mentored seeking out an individual to be a guide. There may be the transmission of advice, but that's not the tone of the word 'mentor'. It is, rather, a sharing of life experience, by two individuals, one more mature, experienced, and wiser, and the other one deliberately latching on to this more mature individual to help himself or herself develop more. Finally, before we start looking at the aspects of mentoring, we have a sense of informality. *We may be assigned an adviser. We choose a mentor.*

What characteristics should the mentor NOT have?

Asking about the characteristics of a mentor is like asking a person about the characteristics of one's beloved. What characteristics should my beloved have? Put that way, the question can't be answered. Because mentoring is so personal, we really should not choose to define the mentor himself, but rather attend to the process. It's always easier in such truly delicate situations.

On the other hand, and there's always another hand, one can go through a list of characteristics that that mentor should not have, or better, a list of characteristics that are usually not associated with mentoring. So here's a list of some of the 'bad stuff', the anti-mentor qualities:

1. <u>Self-centeredness</u>. A mentor has to give of himself, share parts of his soul. A self-centered person might be a friend, but it's hard to imagine such an individual having sufficient generosity to share. A person who is self centered can't really go outside of himself to think about the mentoree as anyone but merely a separate individual. It's hard for the self-centered person to feed another's soul when he can't see, or when he is incapable of acknowledging the needs of the other.

2. <u>Under-developed empathy</u>. An adviser doesn't have to like the advisee, nor even tolerate for more than a few moments. Not so with the mentor. The relation between the mentor and mentored is more intimate. A person can sense when he is liked or disliked. A mentor who dislikes his mentored cannot really

do the job. The relation reduces to that of an advisor, which is ok, but not really as productive as it could be.

3. <u>Immaturity.</u> A mentor develops into a role model. An immature person cannot be a role model. There's simply not enough *gravitas*. The mentoring relation may begin with the mentor being immature, but the relation will soon deteriorate because the mentored soon realizes that something is not right.

4. <u>Inexperience.</u> Mentors are important because they have the requisite life and professional experience. It stands to reason that a person inexperienced in the areas to be mentored cannot be a mentor. Of course that sentence sounds tautological, but its not. The mentor need not be a widely experienced individual, long in tooth, great in years. The mentor should simply be more experienced, indeed far more experienced than the mentored in the specific area. Of course if the mentored wishes guidance in life, it helps to work with a mentor who has 'been around', who 'knows the ropes', knows what to do. On the other hand, the mentoree may wish guidance in a specific area, in which case the mentor might be just a few years older. It's the specific experience and guidance being sought.

<u>Down to brass tacks - On what specifically do you mentor?</u>

What's the content of mentoring? Is it specific knowledge, stuff, ideas, the grist of knowledge? Is it style? Is it general principles? The answer is it's all, or some, or occasionally none of the above. There are no written rules of mentoring, no Machiavelli's Prince to guide us. Mentoring is a 1;1 relation that takes on the infinite variety that most close relations can assume. And in that variety lies the stuff of mentoring.

Mentoring typically begins with something professional. Those who want to be mentored don't come with questions about life itself. Such profound questions must wait. The mentoring relation begins as any relation does, with the two parties emotionally distant, and dealing with each other in terms of specific issues. At this early stage the relation is really one of advising.

At some point, the future mentoree will make known the fact that he or she wants more from the relationship. Guidance alone is too impersonal. The 'more' is connection, guidance about a range of things, many to do with personal goals. It is at this point that the relation changes. Each party acknowledges that one will be the mentor or guide, the other the mentored or guided. And, the two parties know who is who. There is no ambiguity; at least not yet.

<u>The value of a mentoring relation</u>

Young professionals in the world don't really know what's going on. Certainly they can talk among themselves. Certainly they have seen their professors, in class, but probably in the laboratory, and in some happy cases at professional meetings. Most aspiring young professionals talk with each other, trying to figure out what's the right thing to do, the right goals to have, the right way to comport oneself.

It is at this inquiring stage that mentoring has its greatest effect. The mentoring relation is a relaxed one, with the mentor clearly taking delight in the mentored and in the developing the relation between the two. It's a chance to inspire a new soul, and in some cases to experience rebirth and redemption. Although one thinks of the mentored as receiving much of the benefit from the relation, the mentor receives a great deal. Rebirth and redemption of one's soul through giving to another is a powerful affirmation of the value of one's life and education. Choosing a mentoree is having a child to mold, a mind to help create, a soul to nourish.

In the end, there's nothing quite like it. Through this unique, intimate guidance the mentored imbibes the soul of the mentor as surely as the mentored learns the ins and outs of the professional. The mentoree is the spiritual and intellectual legacy of the mentor. It is here that the cow gives more freely than the calf can ever take.

The bottom line to all this? Very little in one's professional life can bring so much joy in years to come, long after the mentor has become a colleague and friend. So try it. If you're a student, seek a mentor. Make yourself a mentor, since they are not easily found. And, if you are the senior in the party, open your heart to mentoring. Just try it..and sit back in the knowledge that are in intimate converse with the generations to come, those who will benefit from you through your mentoree.

By the way, it's simple. Just open your heart, and stop thinking of your *amour propre*. *In the world of the noble soul, mentoring surely has a high station.*

✵ ✵ ✵

CHAPTER 4

NAGGING EMOTIONS – COPING WITH THE BAGGAGE OF YOUR EARLY CAREER

<u>Introduction</u>

A lot of this book is given over to the professional side of one's (really YOUR) early professional life, the defining moments of your career when you metamorphose suddenly from one state of unwashed youth into the next state of professional journeyman (or journeywoman, don't forget PC), and then onto that blissful state of professionalism where you get to see what's really happening.

It's a good time to step back and to look inside, at yourself, at some of the feelings you may have, and what these mean. Of course this book is not a self-help book. There doesn't seem to be much point in writing a saccharine book to prepare you for a professional life. You have to live it to see it, and then you'll 'get it'. No royal road of fulsome psycho-babble here. On the other hand, there are feelings which will assault you. It's impossible to know your particular feelings without discussing them, but from many conversations over the years, many of us, long-term professionals in science and business, have come to realize that there are a number of them worth exploring. Not worth solving, nor allaying in a short book, with unknown reader, but worth merely exploring. So, let's go.

<u>Am I just a faker?</u>

Do you remember the time when in college you realized that you were going to go on to become a professional of one or another sort? Did you have the feeling that somehow you were getting into a hole deeper than you realized? If you're reading this book, then probably you didn't rescue yourself then when you could, but rather continued on your way, dutifully finishing college, perhaps going on to graduate school, proving yourself, receiving the degree and then beginning your first job.

Aside from elation that comes with the realization that '*I can actually support myself,*' what else did you feel? Was there a feeling of '*this is me*'? When asked that question, a lot of colleagues shook their heads, and with smiles, 'fessed up' to the fact that when they were awarded their degree or when they began their job, they felt like fakers, phonies, and so forth. And quite a few, especially those who went through the Ph.D. in experimental psychology at Harvard with your author, confessed that they felt that sense of 'faker' or 'phony' even during their graduate student days. Of course no one then would admit to feeling that way, a faker, a phony, 'what am I doing here?', but some 40 years later the confessions spilled the beans. The confessions didn't have to be extracted with anything more than the simple question 'How did YOU feel those days, so long ago?' for poignant memories and stories to burst out, with a powerful suddenness, as if the answerer were reliving the answer in all vividness, there and then.

This feeling of being a 'faker', a 'phony', someone who doesn't belong, appear to be a great deal more widespread than any of us realized. No one who we talked to reported that he or she 'sensed' that this feeling of 'faker' was shared by anyone else. Indeed the 'faker' feeling seemed so shameful that it had to be hidden from the other people, and especially friends and advisory committees. That is, the feeling seemed to be individual, not something shared with others as part of the course.

> *The feelings of falseness are quite different from the types of competence-feelings engendered in medical schools, dental schools, and law schools, where efforts are made to teach each person that he or she is a professional already, just a few years away from actual recognition, but a professional nonetheless.*

And such feelings lead to the next topic, the sense of loneliness.

All alone am I, since I said goodbye, to that comfortable position I had

Actually, the words to the title of this section are from a famous song by Brenda Lee, the short bombshell singer in the early 1960's who mesmerized all of us who were her fans those many years ago. Just a short introduction to Brenda Lee, pulled off U Tube in May, 2009:

> *Brenda Lee - an awesome, natural talent. No female singer today comes even close. This is a great example of hitting the note, knowing how much inflection, etc. The 'divas' of today could learn a lot from this woman.*

And now the words, which could be transposed quite simply to represent not so much the loss of love as the loss of innocence upon going from a well-ordered college life to the lonely life of the prospective Ph.D.

> *All alone am I ever since your goodbye*
> *All alone with just a beat of my heart*
> *People all around but I don't hear a sound*
> *Just the lonely beating of my heart*

But just what is this loneliness? Certainly the graduate student or the young professional is not really alone. There are other classmates, other individuals who can be easily observed to be going through the same process. The loneliness must be something different, something far more profound.

Perhaps the loneliness is the foreboding sense of going on the hero's journey.

The sense that what is about to happen is no longer a game, but the essence of life's passage. Perhaps loneliness is really that first inkling of real adulthood, and perhaps the intuition of death, the end, at the finish of the journey that one is now commencing. It's not easy to grow up, or grow old.

Whatever it is, the feeling of loneliness is real. It seems to be more real for graduate students than for medical, dental, law, and other students of professional schools. Perhaps that's because graduate schooling is, at its very core, a very different journey than professional schooling. In graduate school students are encouraged to 'choose the road less taken'. And 'that makes all the difference' (adapted from Frost's poem, The Road Less Taken).

Sunday nights

We move from the sublime and general emotions to the more idiosyncratic ones. The emotion in this section we label Sunday night. It is a feeling, often not particularly well articulated, about Sunday night being different, being sad, being *time out of joint*. And, of course, Sunday night is idiosyncratic. There is no reason for any night of the week to be different, special, and call attention to itself. Yet Sunday night does. Why?

In western business the work-week begins on Monday, as does the school week. This means that Sunday night becomes the *de facto* dividing line between the 'fun' of the weekend and the 'work' of the week. But, it's not the Sunday night itself that's the problem. It's one's fundamental feeling about relaxing versus working.

Many colleagues mentioned that vague feeling of dis-ease on a Sunday night, but for different reasons

1. To some it was a sense that the weekend was finished, and they would have to return to work Monday. That's pure and simple. They enjoyed the weekend, and now they were going back to something less enjoyable.

2. To some it was the exact opposite. This second group of people reveled in work. And so during the weekend they were left at 'sixes and sevens'. Certainly there was stuff to do, chores to do, things around the house, things to take care of in one's personal life. But, there wasn't the psychic high that came from work, the adrenalin pumping, the excitement of the chase, the positive rewards from work. To this second group Sunday night was lonely, but it would lead to Monday, and relief from whatever anxiety being away from work had managed to manifest itself over the weekend. The loneliness was over. The work week would start.

3. Then there was the most interesting group, those who traveled a lot, and had to leave their homes on Sunday evening to get to their assignment and begin Monday morning. This demand to travel on Sunday means that Sunday afternoon or evening comes to signify an enforced separation from one's family, a line that is crossed from a family life to a solitary week at work. For the author, who experienced that life for a year when starting in the market research industry, Sunday nights forever after that experience came to evoke a particularly sad emotion. Even decades later when it is necessary to travel for business, and to be alone on a Sunday evening, the same feelings burst forth, with the same sense of aloneness, sadness.

Achievement envy - accountability versus countability

As a professional and business person you are judged on what you produce. We all hear of the noble desire to produce only the best. How many of us ever hear advertisements which talk about mediocrity, about average, about fitting in with the crowd? About not raising one's head, because those are the first to be shot at. How often do we hear about the possibly foolhardy heroes, who die, and those equal but opposite perspicacious cowards who survive. Not often, at least not in public. And, the company that advertises that its products are about the same as everyone else would, and gets away with what it can in terms of product quality, would be laughed out of town, be the joke of the industry.

But what does this have to do with what you produce? Unfortunately for us the world focuses on amount that one produces, on what survives, not the nobility of what one produces. Of course it's nice to talk about the quality of what one produces, but quality is hard to measure. So understanding this notion of countability of work product is important. It's here that knowing about people really counts, because its people who make the decision.

And so this section on countability, where we deal with the emotions which accompany people in a world of counting professional productivity, and the competitiveness which comes out when people compare their achievements to gain some reward. This comparison generates what might be called 'vita envy', a term first heard about 38 years ago when the author had a chance to work with a number of other promising young scientists, one of whom was Dr. Judith Rodin, later President of the University of Pennsylvania, and now as of this writing President of the Rockefeller Institute in New York.

Starting the counting process – go to the stelae (monuments) of publishing

Look at the biographies of people in business, and then look at the biographies of people in research. Begin with the short biographies in social networks, such as Linked In®, which allows business people to see the achievements of others. With Linked In®

you can scan a person's biography in less than 30 seconds. You will discover where the person worked from the start of the career to the present, see what the person's title was, and finally learn about the person's responsibilities and accomplishments. That's it, one page, summarizing the entire person. Most of the bios will follow this format. The reason is simple. For business, the objective is *what can you do for me*'. The resume talks about one's achievements, and the level of accountability that one had in business. Finally, there is no emotion really in reading. There may be curiosity (what was this job really), there may be social geography (did this person know XYZ, my friend in the company at the time), and there may be some detective work (what's this pattern really telling me about this individual). But at the end of the day, the resume on Linked In®, or the standard one page resume communicates what the resume holder can do for the prospective employer or business associate. There's no emotion in the resume, other than a clearly polished attempt to be authoritative, competent, and soothing.

☆ ☆ ☆

Now let's move from the world of business to the world of the academic, to the academic resume, the cv, curriculum vita. We find in academic resumes a rather different set of entries, designed to provoke other emotions along with simple competence, which these resumes certainly do. Whereas in a typical non-academic business resume we find a list of jobs with their increasing level of responsibility which in turn instills confidence, we find in the academic resume more of a sedimentary rock, with its layers of deposits, year after year, painstakingly detailed as if one were preparing it for a legal affavidit.

The academic's resume begins with the jobs. But, the real objective is to lay out one's achievements, achievement after achievement, in a painstaking, agonizing detail. These details include books published, refereed papers published, followed by book chapters, conference papers and abstracts, and of course presentations given. At the end of the day the academic resume is designed to evoke different feelings; not so much a sense of confidence in the person that the person can do a good job for the individual doing the hiring, but rather that the person is solid, and substantial. But feeling of solidity, of substantiality comes from the display of all achievements, rather than of individual jobs held. It's sort of like the aria in Aida where Egyptian general Radames leads a triumphal march, followed by all the wealth he conquered. In the end the larger the resume, the more that it's packed with text about papers and so forth, the more insecurity and even jealousy the resume provokes in the person who reads it.

Of course one can't change the way resumes are written. And, in actuality, the business resume is written for a different purpose. The business resume is written for the person as that person interacts with an employer. The academic resume is, in contrast,

an ongoing monument, a paper-based stela, to the individual academic. As Wikipedia®
explains (Italics mine)

> *The erection of steles was popular in China and consisted of rectangular
> stone tablets usually inscribed with a funerary, commemorative, or edifying
> text…..the design of steles drifted away from pure Buddhist influence and
> became wordy displays of script mostly eulogistic or commemorative. They
> were placed in front of tombs to announce the name of the person buried
> there, often to provide details of the deceased's life, or were provided to com-
> memorate a particular incident or event and to give details of the purpose
> of the occasion. Erecting steles at tombs or temples eventually became a
> widespread social and religious phenomenon.*

Summing up

Your early career remains with you. Whether you go immediately into professional research in the university or in business, you begin alone, without a real support
network. It's just the way the field you chose happens to work. It's a lonely field. And,
as you persist in the field, moving from proving yourself to establishing yourself, you
discover ways of coping.

The loneliness remains, however. The business person with a scientific background
moves out from the early days of a career by taking on greater and greater responsibility. The cv, the resume reflect that growth by increasingly important jobs, and job
titles.

In contrast, the academic measures out his life differently. For most professionals in
the academic world the measure is number of achievements, a sort of sedimentation
of one's life into layers of limestone, and eventually more impressive layers of marble.

✫ ✫ ✫

CHAPTER 5

ON BEING ALONE

Who of us has not had the feeling of being alone, of being isolated, away from others? The sense of being alone can be dreadful. Imagine the young graduate student, away from friends, in a world of 'adults'. Imagine the fear building up inside this graduate student, the sense of inadequacy when confronting older, accomplished professionals. Imagine, perhaps, the sense of feeling false, of 'what am I doing here', and the host of other emotions that surge forth.

On the orientation day of the author's graduate career, in a large room in Memorial Hall at Harvard University, September 22, 1965, Dean Peter Elder of the Graduate School of Arts and Sciences pronounced these wonderfully encouraging words for the incoming students, whose who would later become among the academic elite:

> *Look at the person on your left. Look at the person on your right. One of you three won't be here* (and so forth... the rest is forgotten in the ensuing state of shock)

Forty four years later, it seems from recounting this experience to others, that such 'greetings to the new graduate students' were not only common, but constituted the standard opening to the lonely trip to professionalism. The closest one can get to it would be the definition of the 'hero', who journeys forth from the civilization to an area beyond, and returns later, transformed. Literature is filled with such heroes. A perfect example is the opening lines of Dante's Divine Comedy, where he describes the start of this journey:

> *Midway on our life's journey, I found myself*
> *In dark woods, the right road lost. To tell*
> *About those woods is hard – so tangled and rough*
> *And savage that thinking of it now, I feel*
> *The old fear stirring....*

Translation by Robert Pinsky

Beyond the 2/3 to existential survival

If the mere survival of two out of three were to be the only concern, it wouldn't merit much of a treatment in this book. After all, the passing of one third of the graduate students is not devastating, but merely a statistic, an unpleasant one to be sure, but a statistic nonetheless. A factoid, like other distressing factoids; terrifying at once, and then laughed at, scars of a wound long healed, of a struggle long over.

But we're talking about loneliness, something profoundly deep, something that manifests itself with subtle ferocity during the days of one's graduate career. We don't hear much of this type of loneliness in business school, in law school, in medical school. We hear, of course, about tough times, brutal competition, indifferent academic executions of budding students, but we don't have loneliness. Not really existential loneliness. These professional schools producing managers, lawyers, doctors, public health servants, architects, teachers, are organized into classes, into cohorts, into squads of individuals who will live together, nourish each other, go through basic training and battle testing together. These individuals in professional schools will maintain life-long friendships because they share a common, almost standardized experience as they mature into the professional. They share because they will remember that they 'went through it together', like recruits in basic training, or in officer's candidate school. No loneliness there. Not really. None of the deep, profound angst of the individual as hero, who journeys along away from the world to prove himself, and then back to the world to tell the story and live out his days.

Must it be so?

When the author was a first year graduate student, having come from Queens College in New York City, this notion of being alone in the quest was at first disquieting, almost dispiriting. The 1960's Queens College, and perhaps many other colleges, instilled a sense of camaraderie in its students. Many of the students were preparing to enter law school, medical school, dental school, and the like. Others were preparing careers in accountancy, and still others were preparing for a life in teaching. These individuals in some way 'knew' what they were going to do. Of course they could not know the specifics, the daily routine that each would face, but each had an idea of the type of life to be expected. The key word here is 'preparing'. Preparing means setting oneself up, based on expectations. We cannot call these people 'alone'. Individuals might feel 'alone' in some moments, but the truth is they are a cohort.

Then there were the rest of us. A number of us were planning to go for the Ph.D. Unlike our colleagues preparing for a professional career, we didn't know what to expect. Our professors could be role models, but the truth is, very few of us could imagine what the professor did outside of class. There might be the odd tutorial or project on which we would work for a professor, but we had no clear ideas about what lay ahead. We didn't have expectations, stories, well-trodden paths on which to make our way. In fact, in today's parlance, we might well be described as profoundly 'clueless'.

So here we have two groups. One group, those pursuing professional careers, knows what to do, the steps of the dance, the expectations that will be made of them. The struggles that they face will require them to overcome hurdles, to get into the profession, to imbibe the appropriate knowledge, to display the right capabilities, and finally to be acknowledged. They will have to learn to do what is expected in the profession, to execute specific actions competently, and occasionally with ingenuity. Creativity is not particularly welcome in these professions, although accepted. These individuals, these professionals, belong to the group. They may feel lonely inside, but not because they are on a quest, and certainly not because they are going it alone.

We've just described two different types of education paths. The first path is filled with competitive fellowship. It is the path of the professional school. You're one of a group. You're going through the path. You'll be the class of (fill in the year). Drilled into you day and night is that you're one of a group. In law school and business school you're encouraged to join study groups comprising some of your classmates. In these groups you'll cover for each other, test each other, work out problems, and resolve issues, all in a cooperating group. The covert message is that whereas later on you are going to compete with each other, or perhaps work with each other in one or another endeavor, your professional education should teach you how to collaborate and to support each other. You're one of a group. You have to contribute to the group's health.

What is the other education path? Well, it's a personal path, the path of the graduate student. There may be prescribed courses, certain types of skills that you must evidence, and the ability to write a dissertation. You may see study groups, but not really formalized ones, encouraged and structured by the school. Graduate school education does not consist of a series of skills to be mastered to achieve competence. It's not a question of competence in an area. It's a question of proving yourself against a series of criteria which you, and for the most part even your professors, scarcely understand. Certainly you know the specific steps that are expected to be completed. But, as a graduate student, especially one studying for a Ph.D., it is up to you to carve your own path, make your own way. You may do it as part of a research group, and get your Ph.D. for your contribution. Or you may choose an area and master that area. The fundamental reality here is that you travel alone in this quest, not part of a group, except perhaps as a momentary 'accident' of fate.

Facing the existential aloneness

If intellectual prowess and professional accomplishment are foremost among the stated issues for a scientific (and other higher) education, then existential aloneness is foremost in the unstated issues.

Graduate students pursuing a Ph.D. trod alone on a path. You may be part of the research team, assigned by a senior professor to a group exploring some problem. Yet, in the end, it is a question of carving your own path. And that carving the path means that you have to go into the dark woods of Dante, that world where you will discover nature, and discover yourself. In the very end of your days of education you will be judged by the path you take, by your choices, and by your solo accomplishments.

You might be content simply to teach, in which case your education may in effect be equivalent to a professional certification, much as the M.D. degree is the certification that the person can (eventually) practice medicine. We're all familiar with that path; how many of us have heard that '*I did my Ph.D. and that's the last research I did… we just had to do independent research to get the degree*'. We're not going to deal with that path, because it doesn't really have much to do with the existential loneliness of the scientists.

Now what about the rest of us, the ones who actually believe that a part, and perhaps even the major part of our future, lies in discovering new things through science? How do we face this existential aloneness? Your research work, your efforts at proving yourself worthy of the degree, and later on the research that you take are part of this existential quest for who you are. The most important thing, however, is that when you become a scientist, at least for a short while you take the hero's journey, out from the known.

In a sense that hero's journey into oneself to prove oneself is the education of the budding scientist and researcher. Not so much the coursework, which fills you with the requisite information that you can regurgitate oh so dutifully in your examinations, organized 'just so', with the proper emphasis on theory and facts. No, that's not your education. That's just the stuff which fills your mind. The real education is that alone time, when you grapple with the unknown, put your mark on it, organize experiments, and take a leap into what is unknown. You come back with the Golden Fleece, or some other treasure, and with a melange of observations and intuitions. And, if you do this correctly, you move on to your career, having demonstrated your prowess to wander into the unknown and come back with the (or some sort of) prize.

✫ ✫ ✫

CHAPTER 6

PATTERNS, NOT POINTS:
THE PSYCHOPHYSICAL WAY OF THINKING

<u>Introduction</u>

Now we talk about the issue of actually doing research. It's not an issue here of what comprises an experiment, but rather the *realpolitik* of experiments, how to come up with the designs, and how to make sure that the experiment always works. *Realpolitik* in science is almost always more interesting a topic than the actual experiments themselves, unless of course you're deeply embroiled in your master's, Ph.D., post-doctoral research and thus find yourself in the early stage of your career. At that stage the particulars of the experiment are most interesting to you. We'll avoid those in favor of the more interesting meta-view of scientific experimentation.

<u>Learning to be a scientist</u>

Some time during our formative years, most likely in college although later for some and earlier for others, we are taught about experiments and the scientific method. Most of us don't start out with the discipline of science. It's a bit hard to be a scientist at the age of 17 or so. Of course this notion of the scientific method might be something that can be parroted back on an exam, but it takes years and experience to internalize it so that it becomes part and parcel of one's being.

But just what is this scientific method, and more importantly, how can we use it profitably to understand the world, and of course advance what is most precious to us, namely ourselves? When we're growing up, when we're studying high school science, it's not really clear what the scientific method is really all about. You have be in it to understand it. Wikipedia® puts it quite succinctly:

> *Scientific method refers to bodies of* <u>techniques</u> *for investigating* <u>phenomena</u>, *acquiring new* <u>knowledge</u>, *or correcting and integrating previous knowledge. To be termed scientific, a method of* <u>inquiry</u> *must be based on gathering* <u>observable</u>, <u>empirical</u> *and* <u>measurable</u> <u>evidence</u> *subject to specific principles of* <u>reasoning</u>. *A scientific method consists of the collection of* <u>data</u> *through* <u>observation</u> *and* <u>experimentation</u>, *and the formulation and testing of* <u>hypotheses</u>.

> *Although procedures vary from one* <u>field of inquiry</u> *to another, identifiable features distinguish scientific inquiry from other methodologies of knowledge. Scientific researchers propose* <u>hypotheses</u> *as explanations of phenomena,*

and design <u>experimental</u> <u>studies</u> to test these hypotheses. These steps must be repeatable in order to dependably predict any future results. <u>Theories</u> that encompass wider domains of inquiry may bind many hypotheses together in a coherent structure. This in turn may help form new hypotheses or place groups of hypotheses into context.

Among other facets shared by the various fields of inquiry is the conviction that the process be <u>objective</u> to reduce a <u>biased</u> interpretation of the results. Another basic expectation is to document, <u>archive</u> and <u>share</u> all data and <u>methodology</u> so they are available for careful scrutiny by other scientists, thereby allowing other researchers the opportunity to verify results by attempting to <u>reproduce</u> them. This practice, called full disclosure, also allows statistical measures of the <u>reliability</u> of these data to be established.

The foregoing three paragraphs give a wonderful explication of the method. They give the outline of what the method is, but don't tell you anything about doing experiments. They talk about observation, experimentation and hypotheses. As you might expect if you've ever taken a course in mathematics 'the specific proof (or whatever next step) is left as a proof for the reader'.

So in this chapter we're going to take up the issue of doing experiments. And, since one should limit oneself to one's area of knowledge, we're going to focus on the psychophysical approach to science, which looks for relations among variables, rather than testing the truth or falsity of a specific proposition or conjecture.

<u>Measuring 'points' versus discovering 'patterns'</u>

When we read the history of science, whether natural sciences or the social sciences, we may be struck by the way people talk about 'truth'. There are really at least two clear ways of uncovering the truth. These two ways were brought home to this author in 1969, when working with Dr. Linda Bartoshuk (now at University of Florida and a member of the National Academy of Sciences, then of the US Army Natick Laboratories).

Linda had studied with Professor Carl Pfaffmann at Brown University, during the 1960's, and was one of the earliest researchers in the modern day psychophysics of taste, as was the author. Our lunch time conversations, often including a third member of the research team, Dr. Herbert Meiselman, also of Natick Laboratories, often dealt with the meaning and approach to science. What was the right thing to study? What was worth spending time on? How would we know what was true, and what was not? What would make a lasting contribution?

The foregoing questions are important questions, hardly answerable by young scientists and the early part of their careers. Yet we pursued the discussions because we were all sympathetic to each other, being psychophysicists, but each coming at scientific truth from a unique perspective. Quite a lunch merry go round it was, and would be for a year while all three of us worked together.

But to get on with the meat of the matter, rather than the reminiscences (which, parenthetically, are delightful to recall and to set down on paper). The essence of our discussions was how to conduct science. Linda came from what we might call a 'hypothetico-deductive' background. The bottom line was that for Linda, science was a series of more or less connected ideas about how the world 'might work'. These ideas suggested underlying 'mechanisms'. For example, for a specific taste to be recognized, the 'mechanism' might be that the tastant molecules somehow binds to a specific receptor on the tongue, the nerve innervating that receptor would fire, and the brain would somehow recognize which nerve was firing, and through proper coding, would recognize the taste.

In the hypothetico-deductive system there are a lot of connections, suppositions about how the mechanism is actually constructed. The important thing for us, however, is that the system produces certain predictions of what would happen. Researchers can test those predictions. When the predictions are proved false, the experiment nullifies the hypothesis, and something new, albeit of a negative nature, is learned. When the experiment proves out, and the expected consequences are observed, this chain of facts comprises empirical evidence that the hypothesis possibly might be true. Philosophers of science and logicians, as well as empiricists know that confirming the prediction doesn't confirm the hypothesis, but just strengthens the feeling that the world might work that way. What we just described, the method of coming up with guesses about how the world works (more elegantly described by the word hypothesis) characterizes most of the scientific thinking in the world.

The hypothetico-deductive method is attractive, not because of its catchy and zippy name (!), but rather because it produces a body of ideas, which when linked together, tells us how the world works, or might work. We have a sense of the world as a machine, and we feel that we know what's going on. We step from stone to stone across a river, as we move across, with each stone comprising part of the path. We experience minor euphorias as we string together these confirmed hypotheses, because over time they blend together and begin to tell the 'story' of nature in a way which makes sense. We find patterns as we fill in the story. It's all very emotionally rewarding, to fill in the holes, and see the story of nature emerging in front of our eyes. Who could resist?

The foregoing paragraphs describe Linda's point of view, and most of Herb's. The goal was to uncover mechanisms, to learn how nature 'worked', to get a sense of what reality was all about, and to make a mark by discovering some of these mechanisms.

Then there was your author, Howard. I had a different world-view from Linda and Herb, despite our all receiving Ph.D.'s in experimental psychology. It was the deeper grounding a few years before in mathematics, when I studied math intensely at Queens College, in New York City.

During the middle and late 1960's I was privileged to study with S.S. (Smitty) Stevens, at the Laboratory of Psychophysics, in Harvard University. We were all psychophysicists, Linda, Herb and myself, so the education that I had in psychophysics isn't what separated our minds, and led to the discussions. It wasn't psychophysics at all. Rather, it was a way of thinking.

According to Smitty, the best research involved the careful search for *relations among variables*. That was appealing to me, perhaps because of the deep grounding in mathematics. There was no need for hypotheses about how the world worked. In Smitty's terms, put as one of the leading quotes of his Handbook of Experimental Psychology (1947), '*theories abound in the absence of fact*'. That phrase about said it all, but of course it would be 40+ years until the reality and perhaps wisdom of that phrase would sink in.

In Smitty's world, knowledge wasn't created by testing the validity or invalidity of a hypothesis, a one-off research event. In Smitty's mind, people began to believe that this is the way the world just might work, and spent all their time proving or disproving certain connections, which were the scientist's hypotheses. In the same vein, Smitty felt that those interested in neural processes were also thinking about the brain and neurophysiology in terms of boxes, and processes. All of these efforts, interesting and making great fun for reading, weren't really science, but rather mythology.

How did Smitty's world-view manifest itself? And what did that world-view mean for what's the <u>right kind</u> of research to do? First, let's talk about the personal interaction, and second we'll talk about the research approach. At the personal level anyone involved with Smitty, as the author was, quickly learned to avoid the notion of 'testing hypotheses'. There may have been a world of testing outside the Psychophysics Laboratory, but this notion of testing was to be left outside. It was pretty clear; no single *experimentum crucis*, no one demonstration would suffice to show how nature worked. It simply wasn't the way, or more politically correct, is wasn't his way.

That was Smitty in a nutshell. But what then were the positives? It's not sufficient to denigrate another point of view without offering a counter. In Smitty's didactic manner, the effort was always made to ask for the 'right answer'. The notion of a 'right answer' in science seems a little judgmental, and anti-intellectual. However, in retrospect the idea of a 'right answer' means '*did you uncover the correct relation?*' The key word is 'right', or later on 'correct'. Science wasn't an exercise in statistically affirming or rejecting hypotheses. That was too subjective. Science was a matter of extracting through experiment the rules of nature, lawful relations which undergird the reality in which we live and operate.

Now, let's look at Smitty's version of science from the practical point of view. What does it all mean? At one level it means looking for the 'right answer'. But, as we all know, we won't truly learn the right answer for a long time. So that's really not what Smitty was after, and in fact it would be rather pointless to look for a right answer.

Another clue to what Smitty wanted, and in fact what informed his thinking and the psychophysical approach, is the search for general patterns. Smitty was fond of using a phrase, almost *ad nauseum*. The phrase, very telling, is *'as a first approximation'*. So there we have two clues. The first is the right answer (could never be found), and the second is 'as a first approximation', which doesn't talk to hypotheses at all, but rather to the trial and error of measurement.

Putting these two words together, 'the right answer' and 'as a first approximation', and we come to a different view of science. Since, according to Smitty, his discipline, colleagues and even antagonists, is the search for contents, for rules, for patterns, regularities if you will. There's no glory in a science of 'might be'. There's all the glory in the hard won discovery of and measurement of patterns, regularities. This is the stuff of science, the search for regularities, understanding nature by making public recurrent patterns.

How to discover patterns

How do you discover patterns? Or, in other words, how might you start to think like a psychophysicist? Even if you don't want to become a psychophysicist, and most don't, it's a good idea to learn some of their approaches. Those approaches lay the foundation for a successful career.

To think like a psychophysicist means to look for patterns between the stimuli that you can control and the responses that you measure. Rather than thinking about differences and whether these differences are 'significant' (whatever that means!), think about the world the way an engineer might think about it, or the way a child thinks about the world. It's simple.

> When I change this (variable), what happens? When I make a systematic change, what pattern do I observe?

The reality of the situation is that this question is fairly easy to answer. We do it all the time when we learn. Think about learning to ride a bike. We make movements, and then consciously correct the movements. Eventually, we learn the patterns; do something, and you get a specific result. Over time and experience, we learn the patterns, we understand how nature works, and we adjust the pattern of our behavior to fit with the way nature works. What could be simpler?

And so to think like a psychophysicist, to discern patterns in nature, is nothing more than the formalized way that we learn most relations. We make measured efforts, observe the response from nature, or from another individual, and then put observations together so that a pattern emerges. We may do the act unconsciously, or at least not looking so much for the pattern as for the momentary success, such as not falling off the bike. But, over time, and with practice we learn the pattern, often so well that we can synthesize the pattern in our minds in a so-called *gedanken* or thought experiment. Psychophysics is merely the scientific equivalent, wherein we try to fit formal mathematical expressions to the relation that we are discovering.

If you really want to think like a psychophysicist, it takes just one more step. The step is to pick some 'continuum' that interests you, such as the value of money. Then, you systematically vary the amount of money, and measure the rating of value. Of course you can do many more fancy manipulations, such as taking back money instead of giving money, or saying that you will give the money in six months, or tack on some probability in each case that the money may disappear instead of being given to the subject. And the rating need not be perceived value; it could be happiness, or willingness to work for the money.

As you read the description of the foregoing, you get a sense that the psychophysicist is not 'testing a hypothesis'. There is no factoid to be demonstrated, which shows the mechanism of psychological utility. The researcher simply maps out the relation between money and utility, in whatever way is deemed appropriate. The real knowledge which emerges from the exercise is the nature of the relation. The additional knowledge might be how this relation varies under different conditions, such as different individuals participating (rich versus poor; male versus female), or different instructions and set-up expectations (the person will receive the money versus give back the money; the person will gain the money but only as part of a gamble which can be lost just as readily as being won). We look for rules, for patterns, for equations. It is those patterns which constitute the basics of psychophysics, and to a psychophysicist constitute the most relevant way to understand how the world works.

The Good News Gospel - Why you won't 'blow it' by looking for patterns

Up to now we have been talking about ways to approach science, whether through the hypothetico-deductive method or through the pattern-descriptive method that one might use in psychophysics. When a younger researcher encounters this argument about the proper way(s) to do science, the argument seems a bit forced, a bit irrelevant. After all, looking at the vast scientific literature which continues to emerge each day, one might think that the matter will sort itself out sometime, and that we're simply 'dancing on the head of a pin', that we're dealing with an arcane topic.

However, there are some interesting applications of the argument about approach to science. And, to make matters more relevant, the applications have a great deal to do with one's success both early in the game and later on. So let's delve a bit more deeply.

We begin our delving by looking at the condition of the graduate student, who is casting around for a topic on which to write a thesis. The topic must be sufficiently substantive to support the extensive work needed for a doctorate. The 'question' being addressed must have scientific merit, and fit into the scientific literature, some-how. The objective now is to find the right hypothesis, or in academic jargon, to 'frame a hypothesis'. (That's sort of like *unpacking* a piece of literature, such as a poem).

This notion of *'framing a hypothesis'* implies that one is going to determine how some of nature 'works'. The notion of the hypothesis implies that there is some mech-anism that the young researcher is going to posit as existing in nature, and then the experiment will either confirm or disconfirm the validity of that hypothesis. The stu-dent's thesis will comprise a series of experiments, emerging from the hypothesis. At the end of the experiments the researcher will apply statistical methods, to confirm or disconfirm the results. What could be simpler?

Actually, there is a simpler approach. Rather than positing 'how the world works', one may take the easier path. That path is to look for a relation between two variables. The *'way the world works'* becomes simpler, more tractable, less formidable when the efforts move to searching for lawful relations between variables. For example, one may look for the relation between the sweetness of a sugar solution and the molarity or percentage sucrose in water. What is the hypothesis? The hypothesis is a general one – that there is a relation between the two, and the research effort will focus on finding this relation.

We can make the search for the underlying relation more realistic by moving out from sugar solutions to cola beverages. We can even invoke greater reality by saying that we will measure the relation between sweetness as the rating, and a host of physi-cal determinants of sweetness on the chemical side, such as sweetener, acidulant (the acid, such as amount of phosphoric acid), color, cloud, carbonation, and so forth.

The research approach is quite simpler, and in fact far simpler than proving a hy-pothesis. The psychophysical approach merely requires that you systematically vary the stimulus so that the variables take on different levels and are not correlated with each other. The response could be a rating, or perhaps some task (speed of pressing a button), or even some non-cognitive response such as heart rate or brain wave action. The measures and thus the result data can then be analyzed graphically to discover a relation between or among variables. Afterwards, the statistically adept can use regression analysis to discover the parameters of the model.

With systematic variation it is quite hard to 'blow it', unless you do a sloppy experiment, so that your measurements aren't precise. However, when you take sufficient care to present the right stimulus to the right person, and collect the rating, you will have done the experiment. Whatever you discover will be a finding!

The next steps are straightforward, and fairly programmatic:

1. When you find no relation between/among the variables, that's a discovery, as long as you controlled the variables and made the proper measurements.

2. Whatever relation emerges among the variables is also a discovery.

3. Once you have uncovered the relation, you should then demonstrate its reliability by repeating the experiment, to show that you got the same result again.

4. Afterwards, you're free to show how the relation changes, or does not change, when you introduce external variables into the system. For example, does the relation between sucrose concentration and sweetness change in any particular way in the presence say of a bitter or salty or sour substance? There are a lot of these parametric investigations you can do, to 'flesh' out your discovery.

Notice that you are not positing something about how the world works, and then rigorously testing your hypothesis. Rather, you are showing how variables relate to each other. From those quantitative relations you can speculate how the world might work. So, in a sense the act of developing the relation is the real science, and the hypotheses that may emerge are the speculation. Contrast that with the ordinary approach that most scientists use. They posit a hypothesis (our speculation), and bring the armory of science to destroy it (confirm versus disconfirm).

Which method is ultimately more productive: the hypothetico-deductive method of speculation and disproof, or the psychophysical method of pattern recognition, pattern expansion and then speculation? The odds are that you will get further in your career by systematic exploration of patterns with *post-hoc* speculations, rather than speculations at the essence of your science and then efforts to disprove or prove the speculations.

Preparing during your education

What should you do to prepare yourself to discover patterns, or to create hypotheses? And, is the education the same for both types of science? Perhaps a better way to state that last sentence is '*are the proclivities for mathematical reasoning the same for those who are attracted to patterns versus those who are attracted to hypotheses?*' What a mouthful!

It would be interesting to study the types of mathematics to which scientists are attracted, and why. From personal experience, calculus and the study of relations between variables was always more intuitive and easier to grasp than say mathematical statistics and probability theory. How one or two variables drove a third was always more interesting and the problems easier to solve, than the problems in mathematical statistics, which in turn seemed artificial. Certainly the math stats problems could be solved, but the answers were not easy to visualize. The solution was forced, mechanical, and did not lead anywhere beyond the solution.

You might ask yourself the same type of questions. Which type of mathematics appeals to you, emotionally, intuitively? When you think of a problem do you think of relations between variables? Or do you think in words, in explanations of how the world works, rather than what precisely is happening? Both ways are correct, but they point to different mind-sets, ways of looking at the world, and proclivities.

And then there is the case of statistics. We're not talking here about mathematical statistics or probability theory to which we just alluded in the previous paragraphs. Rather, we're talking about your reactions to statistics as they are used in scientific articles. When you read the articles (papers as they are known in the profession), what role do the statistics play? Do they make you feel comfortable, that the data are real, the conclusions valid? Or are they just sitting there, taking up space, getting in the way of the description? Or do you find them absolutely irrelevant, and find yourself wishing that the author(s) would plot the data and show what's really going on?

Summing up

We can make a succinct summary here. Psychophysics in its way stacks the deck in its favor. A pattern needs very little work to be established. We're not making a conclusion about nature based on a single point, where hopefully we've measured the point accurately. Instead, it's the pattern itself that is of interest, even without any underlying hypothesis.

✲ ✲ ✲

PART 2

MEETING OTHERS

CHAPTER 7

WHAT TO DO AT PROFESSIONAL CONFERENCES

Introduction

As you finish your thesis and begin your professional job, you may begin to notice that people like to meet. It's one thing to read papers from people, and perhaps even to correspond with individuals whose work you find important or even just plain interesting. It's quite another thing to meet these individuals face to face, discuss problems, and simply get to know them.

Professional conferences provide a wonderful venue for meeting people, especially when you are a 'newbie', just starting off in the field. There are many different types of conferences where you can meet other professionals. These conferences range from the very largest (i.e., the national meeting each year), down to smaller, more focused ones, and down to the much smaller, invitation-only conferences.

How to choose a conference

When you begin your career, it's likely that no one knows you. You may have encountered some well-known professionals in your graduate student days, but the odds are that such encounters will have been quickly forgotten by the individuals who you met. The reason is really simple, unpleasantly so. You were then a graduate student. Virtually all but the most sensitive professionals forget graduate students. The reason is also really simple. Graduate students are, to most professionals, the babies of the field. And, for the most part no one is interested in babies. The babies simply aren't interesting; they bring very little to the 'professional party'. Why spend precious time thinking about them? In the immortal words of Gertrude Stein 'there's no there there'.

So which conferences should you choose? If you go to the very large professional conferences such as the Institute of Food Technologists (food) or the American Psychological Association (psychology), you may well be wasting your time and your money. These conferences have thousands of attendees, and as a young scientist or graduate student you're likely to get lost. Oh, you might say that you will gravitate towards your specialty, but it's likely that even that group of individuals will not be welcoming to you. It's simply too big, and even the small parts of these mammoth meetings are unwieldy.

For your initial forays into meetings, you're probably better off going to more local meetings at first, even if they are general meetings in your area, rather than specific to your research interest. For one, it's less expensive to drive to a local meeting than to fly to a national meeting. Second, the people at the meeting are really local; they're your neighbors. You already share a bond; geography. And, for the most part locals are always interested in networking with other locals. Despite the fact that you are a newbie, people will be interested in networking with you because you're there, you're a neighbor, and it's likely that someday you and the others may do some business together. As a result, most local meetings are more informal, friendly, and far less competitive. It's not a 'meat market' at home as it is in a larger conference..

A little more seasoning, say after a year or two at your first job, or after publishing a paper as a graduate student, you might want to venture off into one of the much smaller ad focused meetings, the ones that are by invitation only. As a newbie you won't be invited by the conference organizer because you're simply an unknown quantity. However, by becoming friendly with someone established in the field, preferably someone who goes to these conferences and publishes papers, you can comfortably work your way into the conferences themselves. Despite the 'by invitation only', all professionals in a sub-discipline, of which the conference is an example, realize that they need new blood, year after year. The professionals in the field who go to these conferences often welcome newbies far more graciously than do the same professionals who find themselves at the larger conference. It's something to do with the intimacy of a small, limited-topic conference, run with people who more or less know each other or have known about each other for years and years.

Presenting – oral or poster?

Until the mid 1970's, most conferences featured a limited number of presenters and a larger audience of attendees. The 'best ratio' (i.e., the greatest number of potential listeners) would be found at the large conferences, when the presenter was a 'draw', i.e., well known. The 'worst ratio' (i.e., the fewer number of potential listeners) would be found at the same conferences, in the early morning around 8 am, during the second and third day, in a breakout session, featuring a dull topic and perhaps an even duller presenter. It was always cause for cheering to present early in the conference, because the hard work of presenting was finished quickly, and of course one could then enjoy the rest of the conference. Furthermore, it was likely that attendees would still be interested in the conference, and not jaded, bored, and simply tired as they would be after a few days of being together, 'working the conference'. Early in the conference but later in the morning was best.

Around the mid 1970's a new phenomenon emerged, the poster session. The poster session comprises a series of vertical boards, around six to eight feet wide, and about 3-4 feet high. The boards are made of cork or some other surface to which a poster or set of papers can be affixed.

A poster session comprises potentially several dozen presenters, each of whom is given a poster board in a specific location, and allowed to present the work in written form for the length of the particular session, which may be a few hours at the shortest to the entire length of the conference at the longest.

With a poster the presenter no longer talks about the work, but rather presents it in a structured, sequential way as a written document. From the program the reader knows where the poster session is to be held, knows who is presenting what, and the location of each presentation in the room. Figure 1 below shows a poster given by the author and Dr. Renata Januszewska and other colleagues from Belgium at a recent 'specialty' conference, the 2009 Pangborn Conference in Florence, Italy. Although presented in black and white, the poster is colorful, presents information in a specific format, and is meant to be read with the reader standing up, about 2 feet away from the text.

A poster given by the author and his colleagues from Belgium at the 2009 Pangborn Conference in Florence, Italy

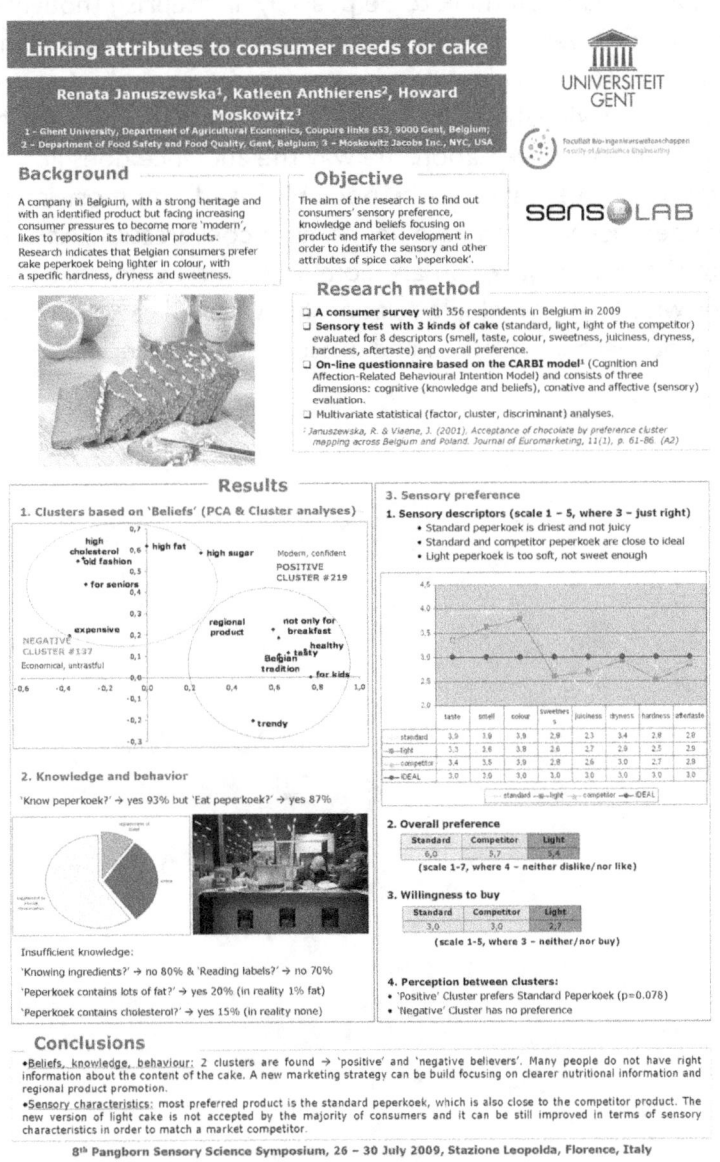

So what's the bottom line about the poster? Let's start with the not so good part, which is mainly ego. Certainly it's not the best thing for one's ego. It's always fun to get up and to present, to hear oneself talk, to feel that all eyes are upon you. Except that that's not true. Anyone who has ever presented in front of an audience soon realizes that for the most part no more than half the audience is paying attention, and no more than half of those paying attention really care. And finally, no more than half of those are relevant listeners. With **48** people in the audience this comes to **6** people listening! So, if you like to speak, posters aren't so good. But, read on; posters are good, and in fact better than good.

There is a very strong benefit to posters, in fact a number of rather pleasantly strong ones. First, when you are a newbie, you don't have to get up in front of the audience and expose what you think to be possibly amateurish thoughts. (They're not, you know, but you don't yet realize it). Second, the poster lets you stand comfortably next to your paper, so that only people who are interested in the topic will come over (see Figure 2). These individuals are motivated to talk to you. They won't go to sleep in the middle of an intimate conversation, the way the audience does at a scientific paper when it is presented by a speaker at the podium. Third, and most important, you get to know people because you can have an intimate conversation. And this is the most important thing, the reason why you are coming to the conference in the first place. It's at the poster where you develop a relationship with colleagues, in a way that would be impossible if you were to stand up and present (see Figure 3).

A typical conference poster room

The author's colleagues at their poster

Even more value from conferences – becoming Sherlock Holmes at poster sessions

A poster session is actually the best place to recognize opportunities for your re-search, and to come upon first order problems. Think about what's happening. Imagine that there are 20, 30 or more individuals who have their work put up on these poster boards, with the work presented in a limited space (see Figure 2 for an example of the way the posters are laid out). The researcher has to make a case for the topic, present the results, and the importance of the results, all in this limited space. So, the researcher makes every effort to condense what will be said and shown to the bare essence of the study. The researcher is putting his or her best foot forward. Poster sessions are thus like speed dating; every attempt is made to emphasize the good.

Now that you have a sense of what a poster is, look around the poster room, such as the room shown in Figure 2. What are people looking at? Are there any posters where people are gathered around, chatting with the researcher, or with each other. Watch the body language. Is the inspection simply cursory, a sort of ho hum nod, or is the reader really interested? Walk over and look at what the reader is looking at. As you observe people reading this and other posters, what do you feel? What do you think attracts the individuals? Is it the problem? Is the method new? Is the poster featuring the fad du jour? Or is there something else going on, a sense of important problem being investigated?

Since the poster session is conducted in public, and since you're allowed to chat with the researcher as well as with anyone else, why not ask other people what they think, or what impresses them. (Try not to be too inquisitive, lest you arouse their irritation, and distress the poor researcher standing at his/her poster, hoping for some positive feedback, and words of encouragement. Give them).

Beyond looking at the poster, look at the other people who you see reading the same poster. Who is looking? Do you see younger people, or do you see older people? Do the people stop and read (especially the older professionals), or do they simply inspect, give a nod, perhaps a shrug or some other cue signaling disappointment or disinterest, and then move on? Watch their body language.

It's important to watch the older people, not the younger people. Younger people in the beginning and the middle of their careers tend focus on the one thing of greatest interest – themselves. So, when you see young people crowding around a poster, its not necessarily the fact that they are responding to a big idea, a first class problem. Rather, it may be that they want to be in the center of 'what is happening'. Create a crowd, and the younger people migrate. They are looking outward as much as inward. They're not good judges of a first order problem, because they cannot recognize one. They're simply not sufficiently experienced.

Now look at the older people, especially those who are well known in the field for their important professional contributions, the doyens. These individuals aren't going to the conference to see or to be seen. They're going to the conference because they are interested in the field, or just as often they are interested in meeting their friends (who with age, dwindle in numbers – conferences are a good place to link up as people move on and on in their lives).

Looking at these older people, watch the posters to which they are attracted, and the ones that they read. When the older individual is truly distinguished, it's likely that the individual will pay attention to important things, and not pay attention to irrelevant thing. Look at what the people gaze on, what grabs their attention. What you discover may well be a good first hint about a first order problem. There is no need for these doyens to dissimulate, to be a poseur, to gain admiration by clucking, by 'ooing' and 'ahhing'. For the distinguished older professional, there's nothing to be gained by phony approbation. So, it's here that you'll find what's important.

✵ ✵ ✵

Walking the conference

A lot of the conference occurs in the hall, not in the poster session, nor in the oral sessions. In fact, it's fair to say that the majority of what goes on really occurs informally, in unexpected meetings outside a 'session' that's going on, or a planned, but short meeting, say for coffee or lunch.

That being said, what is the optimum plan for 'working a conference?' Can you really work a conference, or is it mainly the luck of the draw? Can you increase your success at conferences, and in fact how do you measure success in the first place? There are no metrics of success, so this section simply suggests strategy.

It's best to register early for the conference and show up early, even perhaps a half a day or a day early. This advice may sound a bit unusual, even out of touch, given the very hectic schedules that most people lead, especially young professiojnals who have so much to do.

Yet, there is a reason. Arriving a day early let's you walk around the conference before it is set up, and gives you a sense of the rooms, a feel of the atmosphere. Stop for a moment and think about what's going to happen? What type of conference will it be; big or small, intimate or impersonal? Walking the floors of the conference ahead of time will make you feel more comfortable. You'll learn where the places are to sit and have coffee, so that when you want to meet someone you know where to meet. This is invaluable. You have a limited time at this conference. You're going into 'combat'; knowing the terrain will help you.

Furthermore, by arriving a day early you can get a sense of what the rooms look like, and with that sense see where you want to sit so that you can leave the paper session at any time and return to the room any time you want. There's one other good thing about arriving early. You get to bond with other people who arrive early, or even exhibitors if the conference is a large one, with commercial exhibitions attached. What a wonderful opportunity to hear the latest scoop about what's happening.

Making yourself known but not remarkable

Conferences are a wonderful venue to get known. But, it is important to be known in a positive way, and not just known. Your ultimate goal from the conference is to be noticed, to be thought of positively, to create your own network, and of course to promote your career. So, in light of the importance of these objectives, realize that you will be noticed, no matter what, unless of course you are a shrinking violet who sits in the corner and never utters a peep. And if you are a shrinking violet, then you may well be noticed doing your shrinking because you will stand out from the crowd trying to impress each other.

The devil is in the details. So, what should you do to become known? That's not an easy question to answer because conferences generate a very complex social dynamic. At the conference you will find many different types of people:

1. <u>Young professionals</u>: One group will be the young professionals like yourself, eager to show oneself to the crowd, eager to prove to oneself that one has value by being accepted in conversation among a group of colleagues.

2. <u>Those who are driven, and busy making it</u>: And then there are the middle age professionals, in the midst of their careers, bustling about, surrounded by graduate students, impressing each other (the professionals, not the students!), and very preoccupied being busy. With committees, meetings, more meetings, planned 5 minute encounters, these mid-level professionals are in the midst of 'working the conference' in the most intense way.

3. <u>The grand old folk who haven't yet died or become disenchanted</u>: And finally are the others, the grand old women and men, approaching retirement, happy to be at the conference, not working it, but delighted to see old friends. You'll want to talk to these, not because they can do something for you or recommend you, but simply because you and they are part of the great chain of your profession, and you should know them.

Now that you know the players, how should you behave? That's a tough question to answer. It's important to remember why you are at the conference, and what you want to accomplish. Yes, the conference is about you. But -- no one appreciates listening to a graduate student or a young professional go and on about his work and his deserved, future place in the galaxy. So don't be one of these onerous, self-aggrandizing young folk, filled with himself, and down right irritating. For one, you are probably young yet, and you haven't done the important work in your life. If you have, you're wasting your time at the conference anyway. Second, other people want to hear themselves speak, and by talking on and on you are getting in their way. They don't like it. And third, what you have to say isn't necessarily interesting to anyone but you, your mother, and perhaps your significant other, although even the latter is doubtful.

So back to behaving. It's best to ask questions, and then to shut up. It helps to nod, to pay attention, and to realize that if you are going to succeed at this conference you want people to have a positive attitude towards you. It doesn't help to be the 'smartie pants', the one who is doing it right while everyone else is doing it wrong. No doubt you're in earshot of someone who is 'doing it wrong'.

Listening isn't everything, however. You don't want to be a passive listener. You'll fade into memory in approximately 10 milliseconds after the encounter is over, without leaving a trace. A good strategy, which you ought to prepare for ahead of time, would have you identify say 10 individuals who you know about, but who you may not know. For each of those individuals, write down the particular interest of that person, write down 1-2 questions to ask that person, and then 1-2 points of your own to add to the answer. The person may not even attend the conference, but it's not important. What is important is the exercise itself, play-acting, simulating an encounter and a conversation, preparing a question, and then preparing your own 30 second 'elevator pitch' about your own work *as it connects with the expected answer you will receive*. This 'inner game' is far more important than you realize. By becoming a master at the inner game, by interviewing professionals in your field in your mind and preparing your own additions to the answers given, you'll go a long way towards making the most of the conference.

What if you give a paper and a poorly delivered one?

Shake the hand of a graduate student or a young professional at one of these conferences and you will notice something. The person seems nervous, unsure. Despite efforts to appear calm, many young professionals at these meetings are scared, and for good reason. It is at these meetings where one's image is created, at least in part. There are, of course, many other venues and opportunities besides conferences to craft an image, but its always clearer when you look at someone in your profession and wonder what that person thinks of you, now that you just said something, showed something, presented something.

So now we move to the slightly less pleasant topic, of giving a paper that is not well received. First of all, those of you who are reading, do not despair. And those of you who think you personally have never given a poor paper, don't be so quick to pat yourself on the back.

Giving a poor paper at a conference is done all the time. In fact, and this will cheer you up, more often than not the delivered paper doesn't live up to expectations. The paper can fail for at least nine reasons:

1. Poor and boring topic

2. Incomprehensible speaker

3. Too many tables

4. Hard to read slides

5. Too little time

6. Paper scheduled at the worst possible time (day 2 or 3, early morning, or last day, last few papers)

7. Competing papers of higher quality

8. Competing with social hour

9. Accident at the meeting (projector broke)

Getting the most out of the sessions and the papers

The essence of a scientific conference can be found in the list of papers and plenary sessions. The plenary sessions are large-scale talks presented by a few keynote speakers, who have been invited by the conference organizers with the hope that these 'keynoters', as they are called will spark interest in the conference and increase attendance. In contrast, the contributed papers are often presented in smaller, break-out sessions, more focused, with a limited attendance.

Although a great deal of what goes on in conference occurs in the halls, in informal meetings, it's important to know about the papers in the conference. There are a couple of general facts to bear in mind beyond the specific topics which may be of momentary interest. Knowing these facts will give you an edge.

The plenary sessions usually comprise topics of general interest, and for the most part interest a lot of different people in the audience. Yet, if truth be told, they interest no one very much unless the talks are topical and immediate. These sessions are impersonal. You won't meet anyone at these sessions because most of the conference attendees are sitting at these sessions, or milling about outside. There are simply too many people.

The smaller breakout sessions are more rewarding. Look for the topics that interest you. In the session or, better, just in the hallway outside the session you are likely to find people with similar interests. It's a case of 'birds of a feather'. They tend to be found at the same sessions.

You get more by milling around outside and talking to people than you do listening to the paper itself. Keep in mind that you are attending a small session, with few people, with a paper perhaps given by a graduate student. It's likely that the people can be better understood if you get a copy. (Write to the author, to get a copy of the paper and the slides). You won't get that much from listening to the speaker. The bottom line here – you are at the session to meet people, which is best done outside, and after the session.

If you do find yourself going in to hear papers, you might well consider where you should sit. Although it's often easiest to see the slides when you sit up front, keep in mind that you're likely to be embarrassed when you get up and leave. And you will eventually get up and leave. It's very disconcerting for presenters to see half their audience 'scoot out' at the end of a particularly good presentation, even though one realizes that there is no insult meant. Rather, the various members of the audience have another paper to attend.

When you realize that you too will be 'grazing', listening to papers that you want to hear and deliberately missing those you don't want, the strategic issue is where do you seat yourself in the session? It's usually best to sit near the door, preferably at the back of the room. This way you can leave when you wish. No one will notice you leaving if you sit at the end of the row, right near the door. You can be gone so quickly that the presenter has no idea you were even there.

You will find yourself wanting to leave the presentation for a number of reasons. The most frequent reason is that you find the presentation irrelevant, whether because you aren't interested in the topic, or you are interested in the topic in general but the presentation is awful, which happens far more frequently than you realize. You may also have to take a 'bio break', an especially common reason when you have just drunk a lot of coffee. And, of course, the worst reason is that the room is cold, dark, mostly empty, with a boring topic, and a graduate student struggling to get through. It can be difficult.

Kindness at conferences and, indeed, everywhere; always relevant and important

A hallmark of a career well spent is the nature of how you interact with people. And, continuing that thought, in the professional world where you find yourself kindness should be at the forefront.

You may be asking yourself *'why talk about kindness, and why put a discussion of kindness smack in the middle of a discussion on conferences'*? The reason should become obvious. You as a student or as a young professional are in the early middle of your life. You will be the recipient of many things, ranging from accolades to insults, from kindness to abuse. It's important to remember how you feel when someone is kind to you. But that's just about the acts of kindness.

Now, for the rest of the story. At conferences you have a chance to be kind. There are many students who are looking for a kind word, for encouragement. Just as you need nurturing, so do these students. And, it is at conferences where kindness can shine, where a good and encouraging word can change the life of a student, restore confidence to a despairing young professional. It's good to be kind. And it's good professionally as well. No one was ever disliked because he or she was too decent, said a kind word, acted graciously.

<u>Making a good personal impression at the conference</u>

You've gone to the papers, and of course mingled outside. You've seen people you know, and those people have introduced you to others. You've been quiet and respectful, not too quiet of course. You've let others talk, and nodded your head.

It's important to nod your head in agreement ... get used to it ... it's a way for other people to see that you are listening to their wisdom.

And so it's your turn. You have a minute or two, perhaps more, to make an impression. Your audience may be a colleague about your age and your level of experience. More likely your audience with be a slightly older contemporary, say 5-10 years old, more senior in the field, but not the grand old professional, the doyen. Or perhaps your audience is a doyen, one of the masters, not in the area of your specialty, but someone worth knowing. What do you do?

Well, for one thing, you don't start off with giggles and self-abasement. No one is interested in hearing again and again what an honor it is to meet him or her. Oh, perhaps the first two seconds of such effusive flatter might be nice, but few normal people want to be gushed over. You're not a teen age girl someone with her heart-throb singer just walking into the room.

At conferences most people are self-conscious, recognizing that it's important to put on a good face, to be at the top of one's game, whatever game that may be. So, it doesn't hurt to relax the other person by asking a few simple, easy to answer questions. These are questions of a very polite sort, rather than piercing academic questions. For example, you might ask the other person:

1. How did he or she begin to research the topic area?

2. What was the inspiration?

3. How did it feel at the beginning of the research effort?

4. What were the factors that stood in the way? (This is an especially good question because it lets the other person recall the moments of triumph. Everyone likes to be a hero).

Asking the person about the human emotions he experienced when beginning a project relaxes the other person, and often makes a fine, rather unusual, welcomed interaction. Everyone loves to talk about the softer side of the research, about the emotional connections of the research with some other human aspect. And so, such a conversation produces a wonderful impression in the other person. You are essentially interested in that other person. Finally, it's easy to ask simple questions about the human side of the research. An added bonus here is that the other person may find you much more memorable because there's a sense of 'human connection', rather than the formal interaction that is so prevalent in science.

Try to avoid factual questions of a type that can be answered in a simple sentence. That is, it's really a waste of time to ask more specifics, questions of fact, questions about *what specifically did you do?'* Unlike questions about the feelings when do this, questions of fact don't have a life of their own. They are by nature limited, boring, exclusive, and lead to shut down. The presenter doesn't really want to answer yet more specifics. Finally questions of fact are in some sense implicitly point to the incompleteness of the presentation, a 'no no' when you are trying to establish a positive reputation.

Graduate students are wont to ask statistical questions. 'OY!!!!'. Perhaps it's the noxious adolescent phase of a child's maturation reappearing, this time in the noxious statistical phase of a student's maturation to become a professional. Statistics are a cheap way to score points, but at the same time literally the best way to establish zero memorability. Asking the presenter to justify statistics serves no purpose at all, other than achieving a momentary disequilibrium, as the presenter is pushed into a corner. You'll get the answer, but precious little else. Not what you want to accomplish. And, for the most part, asking a statistical question produces a sense of discomfort in almost everyone in earshot. It's done, but counter-productive. Unless, of course, you plan to establish a reputation as a *'pain in the ass young professional.'*

Meeting someone at a conference – nurturing the relation

If all that happened at conferences were simply chance meetings whose warm feelings evaporate at the end of the conference, then it would be better to save your money or the money of the institution paying your trip. Just stay home, and go to the movies; it's cheaper, less hassle, no discomfort involved. But that's not the case. You probably know intuitively that the meetings you have at the conference can blossom into acquaintance-ships, occasionally deep friendships, occasionally co-authorships, and often love affairs and marriages. More couples meet at conferences than one might think, simply because of common interests. The last point, love, is irrelevant for this book, but not for life.

So how do you progress a casual meeting at a conference to a relationship that may prove life-long, professionally beneficial, and emotionally rewarding? If you've been following the suggestions in this chapter, then you will know to start with a conversation, introduced by a simple, human, warm question. In that conversation you will have asked your prospective colleague (and perhaps friend) about the 'human aspect' of the research, interspersing of course professional observations so the conversation maintains a level of professional competency. The topics surfacing in your discussion, the feelings about specific issues, and especially the emotions involved in certain research endeavors, make excellent points on which you can follow up. Who can possibly resist a reprise of a conversation on the personal aspects of a research project? Keep in mind that when your colleague shares with you some of the emotions surrounding a specific research project, you have been presented with a wonderful entrée to a new person, and perhaps even a new relationship:

1. You know the science of the topic

2. You know the personal/emotional aspects

3. You can provide your own emotional responses to this work or to work of the same type, and later follow-up with a few paragraphs on the science of the research.

The combination of emotions and science move you far beyond either topic alone. The science is the long term glue. The emotions, or the personal aspect of the initial conversation and the follow-up letter provide that 'something' which sets you apart and makes you memorable.

There's only one other topic to deal with in this section on follow-up. And that is, the nature of the follow-up. It's good to follow-up quickly, preferably by letter, but more and more by an email. E-mails are inexpensive and quick. You should attach one or two things which are relevant. Make sure that what you attach is polished, because it will undoubtedly be glanced at the very least. Later on, when you want to follow-up again, you can refer to this email and to your attachment. Furthermore, by enclosing an attachment you have the opportunity to write a bit about the topic of the attachment in the body of the e-mail. The writing moves the email beyond a cursory note into a more thorough letter. And that, again in the words of Robert Frost '*made all the difference*' (The Road Less Taken).

✲ ✲ ✲

<u>Summing up</u>

Conferences are important. *Very important.* Do your homework. Play the inner game. Don't look at conferences as a necessary evil, but as a happy hunting ground where you will 'bag' your future. With this in mind, go to as many conferences as you can. They're worth it – especially at the start of your career. Oh, one final thing. Watch your manners.

✲ ✲ ✲

CHAPTER 8

IT'S YOUR TURN: SEDUCING THE AUDIENCE – ARE YOU A MINIMALIST OR A MAXIMALIST?

<u>Introduction</u>

We live in a world of Powerpoint ®, and Powerpoint® haters. Many of you reading this book will not remember a life without Powerpoint®, or perhaps its predecessor, Harvard Graphics®. To those of you who live in today, and don't know anything else, we'd like to tell you that although you may hear that it's important to have fancy, sexy, zippy presentations, with a website to match, all up to date, the truth of the matter is that content ends ups being king of the hill. And it is content that will occupy most of this chapter, content that you should have, content that you should present, and content that should shape your mind.

<u>What's the goal of a presentation anyway?</u>

When you're asked to present, or when you volunteer (they're quite different), what do you want to accomplish? Sounds like a pretty simple question, doesn't it? Well, ask yourself the question about your last or next presentation. And, without reading further in this chapter, talk out loud, as if you were talking to your mother, significant other, or even better, the snarky, smart 14 year old next door who you've seen develop from a bratty kid to someone with some brains and promise. (Yes Virginia, it happens).

But really, what DO you want to accomplish? Is the presentation a vehicle to show how smart you are, such as what you might present at a conference? At a conference you're ostensibly presenting to share knowledge with your colleagues. More likely, however, and if you're on the youngish side, you're there for a live demonstration of that most important person in the world to you – namely yourself. You never know who is in the audience; your next employer, your spouse-to-be, your professor, or even your mother. So, with that in mind, what do you want to present, and how do you want to present it?

<u>Two styles of presenting</u>

When you attend enough conferences and observe the presenters, you're likely to see at least two different styles of presenting, and hear lots of reasons why each style is the better of the two. The one style is minimalist, the other style is maximalist. Oh, and by the way, you're likely to get an earful why catchy graphics are either wonderful or distracting.

So let's dissect these different styles, trying to figure out what's behind them, what do they accomplish, what's the up-side (you gotta love that word *'up-side'*; not sure what it means) and what's the down-side (that word means it will come back and bite you in the backside).

Minimalists. Like minimalist artists, these presenters put as little text as possible on their slides. A word or two is fine. Even three words are fine. But, beyond that, these minimalists get irritated. Ask them why they like minimalism and you're likely to hear a variety of reasons, all boiling down to the fact that it is THEY who will communicate with the audience. The slides, well they're just an accident, something that one has to do in today's world. The reality, according to minimalists, is the presentation, the panache, the style of delivery, the masterful control of the audience. And, the interesting thing is that many of these presenters actually deliver the goods. They do it in style. But woe be the presenter who attempts to be a minimalist in the text on the slide and yet has no connection with the audience, no power of delivery, no self-assurance no puissance. For in that minimalist presentation lies an eternity. That is, to the audience the presentation will seem like it goes on forever. So, be forewarned. If you are good, go for it, minimize your text. If you are not so good, better have the spotlight on your slides, not on you. You won't be able to fluff your way through it, even with a nervous giggle or two. It just won't work.

Maximalists. To the maximalist the presentation screen (i.e., in PowerPoint) is an arena to feature what will be talked about in that very moment. The maximalist (of which the author is a member, and admits in the interest of full disclosure) does not revel in the audience's attention to himself, nor to whatever showmanship capabilities he has. To the maximalist the easy thing to do is to lay out the slide so that it provides the information that will be presented. Of course the slide should not be dense. There's no really good reason for creating the written paper on a slide. On the other hand, the slide ought to be structured in such a way that the listener who nods off can wake up and read the slide, not having lost much. And the presenter? Well the maximalist presenter really works the slides. The presenter need not read the slide from top to bottom. That would be deadly; sort of the same deadening as reading one's paper. Bad form. However, the maximalist can 'graze' the slide, picking up tidbits here and there. And, there's another benefit as well. The slide presents the information, but also organizes the talk. The presenter only has to remember how to advance the slides.

So by now you're asking – which one is better, please, please, please? Well, there is no answer to this profound question. But, you should look at the way people present, see how comfortable YOU feel with minimalist versus with maximalist slide setups, and then make your choice. The good thing is that you can start out a minimalist, where the presentation is all about YOU deftly working the material. Then, when you get tired of YOU, as your audience surely will, you can revert to maximalist, and let everything 'hang out in the slides'.

One other thing while we're on the topic. Minimalist slides are sort of pointless to distribute. How can the minimalist slide capture the YOU who performs? You are the artist, and the minimalist slide is the canvas without paint. On the other hand, maximalist slides are great. They are sort of the Cliff Notes® to the talk. Like the Cliff Notes® of college days, the slides give the abbreviated version that can be scanned quickly to get a gist of the presentation. The good maximalist presenter can create slides which are both present-able at the meeting, and read-able. Making the slides read-able and interesting means your slides will outlive you. What a thought. And, when you're lucky, they'll be circulated without you even knowing it, creating your reputation while you sleep! Oh happy day.

Graphics and the nature of the presenter

Those of you reading these words who can remember as long ago as 1985, or, perish the thought 1970, will no doubt recall that most of the presentations that people gave were either on lantern slides (big glass slides with a lantern bulb), or 2x2 slides (small, paper bound slides you could keep in your pocket), or transparencies to be put on a transparency projector, and good for the small intimate conferences of your colleagues, or your managers.

What else do you remember about those slides? Or, better, what don't you remember? Well, for one, the slides were effortful to create. You actually had to type stuff or hand draw graphs, unless you were lucky enough to have a CalComp® machine, which would do the onerous drawing, hour after hour, asking you only to fill up the ink reservoir.

There was something else; a lack of graphics virtuosity (or less generously, graphics wizardry). No one really missed graphics. In fact, the audience got along just fine without graphics. The scientists presenting their data would to make sure that the table was readable (not always done), and that the graph was presented in sufficient clarity, without clutter so that the major point would break through. And of course anyone going to a scientific conference would be treated to session after session of these carefully crafted slides. The others, who didn't go to sessions, got to talk outside the presentation room. But essentially no one felt that he was missing a visual entertainment.

And the business people? Well, they also presented their ideas without the benefit of visual entertainment, eye candy on the charts and tables. Of course many of the business people didn't bother with the lantern and later with the Kodak slides. Those were reserved for the scientists, a breed apart. Rather, the business people had to make do with transparencies, taken directly off the paper. Of course there was the signature of the business transparency – it was written horizontally in so-called landscape style. And, it comprised bullets, single ideas on a line, set up to communicate. But, of course, didn't have cute figures and cute backgrounds. In fact, a figure, a cartoon figure, even a picture would smack of something else besides professionalism. Sort of being 'cutesy'; there's not enough gravitas there.

Did lack of graphics make a difference? At least in our minds, those of us who were there, there were no horrid consequences just because the presentation lacked the leg-erdemain of today's graphics design and presentation 'effects'. One didn't end up getting sneered at as an 'amateur' because the slides were too simple. Of course we couldn't really do the controlled experiment, exposing half of the audience to a presentation without graphics but with the relevant material, and then exposing the other half of the audience to the pyrotechnics that PowerPoint® makes available. We don't really know how much more understanding, how much greater audience engagement, how much more fulfilling the time would be had we replaced white space in the transparency with clip art, moving clip art, or even better, a high quality video clip tangentially related to the topic of the presentation. Would the presentation have created greater business demand? Only history could tell us, and unfortunately these wonderful presentation tools (or rather *presentertainment* toys) were as yet not ready for prime time.

On the other hand we have today. Those who are employed by big corporations have the luxury to either send their presentations to an internal department or out-source their presentations to an organization which specializes in making the presentation 'sing'. This singing is accomplished first by changing the template from white to something that communicates the brand. (One must never communicate without emphasizing the brand, or so goes today's wisdom). But that is not all. Rather shortly after that, the presentation is embellished with all sorts of eye candy. It's not enough to have clip art. The art has to move, or even better the presentation has to incorporate high quality video clips. At the end of a 10- slide presentation occupying a little bit of room on one's hard drive we have the evolution into a 30 megabyte presentation (29.9 of the megabytes being reserved for the audio visual). The presentation is too big to send through a normal email, so it's shipped via YouSendIt.com or another such online file transfer utility. And, whereas the old and simple Powerpoint® version (or, heaven forbid, the transparency version) worked quite nicely, now it requires a group of highly skilled technicians to make sure that video clips play.

The bottom line to all of this? Well, if you're going to present, think about what you're going to say. Are you presenting facts? Are you *presentertainment*, showing off the latest oohs and ahs of the PC industry in your talk? Who is in your audience? Does your audience even have an attention span longer than 3 minutes? If so, then you're likely to get more play, and enjoy more success by using your presentation to commu-nicate your ideas rather than to entertain. You're not being paid to amuse.

On the other hand, if you like eye candy, then go right ahead. It's your disk space. And, when there is a group of other *presentertainers* in the audience, you can spend the precious time after your talk comparing notes on the latest and greatest programs to add to your Powerpoint® prowess. You won't get the serious, profound, thought-filled questions, however. Not really. You'll get excited questions, but excited because of the audience's 'sugar high' from the eye candy.

<u>Hearing yourself talk</u>

Think back to the time when you were a young college student or graduate student. Can you remember tests where you didn't know much, and decided that the best way to pass the test was to write as much as you can about the topic? And so, you filled so-called blue book after blue book. The blue book was the small, blue covered, note book that you would use for your tests. You'd write your answers freehand, in essays, in the book. And, the idea of four or five blue books, or whatever number you want to substitute, is a metaphor for the strategy that when you don't know, write a lot. The answer will be 'in there' somewhere. You hope.

And so we move from those agonizing moments of test-taking to equally agonizing moments of presenting. You can usually tell the novice presenters apart from the professionals, not so much by the demeanor of the presentation, but rather by what the presenter will present.

The qualified, experienced presenter realizes that the presentation is not a star-chamber inquisition, and should therefore not be treated as such. It's not particularly productive to be 100% prepared, and indeed over-prepared with all of the possible data. There are going to be negative audiences, but the presenter should not come with a presentation which overwhelms, with all possible data analyses, available 'just in case'. While clearly reducing anxiety through pointless busy work, this mega-defensive strategy won't really pay out in the world of business.

So what's the bottom line here, for the new presenter? There are 12 good points to think about. They're not written in stone, and for heaven's sake, they're not the end all and be all. They are opinion, albeit well founded opinion:

1. You're not that important. What you say in a meeting probably will be forgotten, pretty quickly, and perhaps as you are speaking. That should be sufficiently sobering to you to allay any fears.

2. For the most part, you're not facing enemies. Your biggest enemy is disinterest, and lunch.

3. It's not about you, it's about your topic. No one stands in judgment except your own fears. Most of your audience has already been bored to death over the years. If you screw up the presentation, it's not so bad. No one will remember anyway.

4. Less is more. Get to the 'meat of the presentation' quickly. No one wants to hear all the minutiae of why you should be permitted to present what you're presenting. Again, it's not about you. It's about your material.

5. Talk clearly and slowly. Don't cram in everything.

6. No one knows statistics. It's no damned good going over the statistics. People want stories. What happened? What's the meaning of all the stuff you're presenting? When you can tell a story you're way ahead of the game.

7. Write out your story up front, in the middle, at the end. In bullet points. Assume that no one will remain awake throughout your presentation.

8. Look for signs of 'glazed over' eyes. These are people who have tuned you out. Get them back in by cycling back to the start, and reiterating why what you will tell them will help their business or science. You're not presenting in a linear progression. You can jump back and reiterate, emphasize, repeat, restate in different words. You won't bore anyone.

9. Have content, and don't giggle. No one is interested in the fact that this is your first presentation, that you are nervous. Don't ask for forgiveness, nor call attention to whatever inadequacies you have. The audience will find your inadequacies, even if you don't call attention to them. But..to your surprise... most of the audience just doesn't care.

10. Just relax, and have a good time. If you enjoy your presentation, the others will. Some may even wake up.

11. Talk like you're talking to a friend, telling a story. Don't try to sound like an officious adult. Ugh.

12. A sobering thought is that in your presentation only about ½ the people are following. The other ½ are dozing, checking email, etc. Among the ½ who are paying attention, only ½ of those (i.e., 1 out of 4) is really following you. Among the ¼ who are following you, only half, or 1 in 8 is really interested. So, you've got 12.5% of the room. With 24 people in your audience, only three are tracking you. Is it worth getting worried for a measly three people?

✲ ✲ ✲

CHAPTER 9

ON PROFESSIONAL SOCIETIES;
OR, IF YOU WANT TO BE ALONE, THEN JOIN THE CROWD

Introduction

Let's face it. Birds of a feather *do* flock together. And, in the same way, people in the same field like to flock together to meet each other, to compare notes, compare achievements, even to compare disappointments. And, so we get to the topic of professional societies; not so much how to behave in a professional society or how to get the most out of the meeting, but simply what's the real 'scoop' here? What's going on when professionals begin a society, when senior and junior professionals meet, and even what's happening when the professional meeting begins to evolve, inviting suppliers and other vendors to the meeting to open booths and hawk their wares?

Professional societies don't typically begin in a rational way. Having been at the founding of a number of these societies, we can say for certain that these societies begin as dreams in the minds of a few people. It's rarely one person who dreams up the society. Rather, what seems to happen is that a group of individuals, generally in different but related fields of research, will have met one another during the course of several years, typically at various conferences. Some of these individuals may have studied with the same professors, some may have published with each other, but whatever the connection, these individuals feel a kinship to each other.

After years of attending meetings with each other, some of these professionals may happen upon the idea that in reality this group of like-minded individuals comprises an informal but relatively connected group of professionals, which now needs to establish its own identity. Notice that the emphasis here is *after years* of attending meetings. The society does not spring fully formed like Athena from the head of Zeus, although years later it may seem that way. Rather, the society begins as a group of individuals with different points of view, different hopes, needs, and visions.

From the perspective of the bigger conference, the group will be seen to be heterogeneous, comprising individuals from a variety of seeming unrelated disciplines. Yet to these members of the nascent organization, the connections among the individuals are crystal clear. They all focus on a common science or common topic. Over the years, the author has been present at the formation of societies dealing with new product development (culminating in the PDMA, Product Development and Management Association), sensory measurement (culminating in the Sensometrics Society), individuals dealing with eating and tasting (culminating in both ACHEMS, Association of Chemosensory Research Science, and in SSIB, Society for the Study of Intake Behavior). And the list of societies goes on and on. The general pattern is the same, again and again. The specifics differ, as they must, because specifics come from people.

Evolution

What's interesting about these societies is how they form and how they evolve. Nature doesn't stand still, nor do people, nor do professional societies. And it will be in this evolution that the student and young professional have the opportunity to make a lasting mark.

At the start of the professional society, its moment of conception, it doesn't really seem like there will be a society at all. To be sure, the individuals who comprise the nucleus of this yet unborn organization are profoundly interested in their topic. By the way, there is one other thing that will become increasingly relevant over time. These founding mothers and fathers of the society are not 'politically focused', at least not yet. They may realize that some benefits will come from this new society, but for the most part, the drive to create the society comes from the noblest of motives, and perhaps a bit from the frustration of not exactly fitting into the mainstream of their fields. It is idealism, not *realpolitik*, which rules these early days.

The society often begins as a small satellite meeting within a larger conference, when the idea dawns on everyone that there ought to be a society. It's sort of like Judy Garland who said to Mickey Rooney 'Let's put on a show' in their 1930's and 1940's pictures. The idea seems very reasonable, and a group of individuals, generally the younger ones (ages 30-40 or so) , hurriedly get together and start planning.

Soon, whether it be six months, a year, two years, but in a reasonably short period of time, the society takes shape. Everyone wants to participate. There is a sense of camaraderie, of sharing in the formation of this new organization. Many of the members project their own personality onto the society. For the most part, the early years are lots of fun. It's the newness of the project, the unspoken, but deeply felt hope that through the success of the society, one's own success will be assured. All of these conspire to make everyone happy and enthusiastic to contribute. All beginnings are sweet, or so it is said about love affairs. And so, it is with the founding of the society. What sweet days and what wonderful memories!

We have problems, honey

All good things end. The honeymoon days of a society also have to end. Perhaps, in fact, these wonder-filled honeymoon days end even sooner than expected when a society is formed. The reason is simple. Professional societies, unlike marriages, are organizations created for the convenience of individuals who in other contexts would be competitors, and who, quite often, are professional combatants, even enemies. How could such a marriage last?

But the organization does take shape. When the honeymoon finishes and the idealism has evaporated, the members are left with a valuable piece of real estate – the organization itself. Smart professionals realize that they can push their own agendas, seize power, and use the organization to further their own aims. A professional clique which grabs hold of the society can use it to bring in its students, give choice keynote addresses to their buddies in the field (eminently qualified, of course), and, in general, move the agenda towards the interest of the clique. Other cliques, with just as talented members, but which ended up not having the power in the society, find themselves accepted for papers, but not invited the organizing committee.

All in all, it is an interesting mix. But it doesn't end there. So far ,we've been talking about competition among 'colleagues' in science. What happens when we mix venality into the soup, and allow people to talk about projects in which they have a monetary interest? Then, things really get interesting, as we see below.

Homo economicus – the fox in the chicken coop

Professionals forming an organization may begin with the same dreams and eventually-to-be-realized aspirations of young researchers, with wide eyed hopes and the moral rightness that characterizes the young, just-minted Ph.D. The society is new, it lives, finally! But what happens when money gets mixed in, when *homo economicus* starts to play a role? And, what happens when the professional objectives of the society are interwoven with the financial interests of people who want to sell to the society's members?

Ask a young scientist about the role of money and, for the most part, you'll get either a quizzical look or outright disdain. Yet, it's money that makes the world go around, money that funds the society, money that drives the complimentary registration given to the young researcher, or pays for the long trip for the keynote speaker, who otherwise would remain in his or her laboratory, in splendid isolation, just wishing that someone would call. And so, after a year, or two, or three, or however long it takes, the management of the professional society realizes that economics has to make its entry. It's no longer 'love in a hut'. The society is a year or two old, there are bills to pay, the excited volunteers of a year ago who were wildly in love with the idea see that that reality is a bit duller. It's not the wonderful meals where they are discussing the society; it's doing the damned dishes to keep the society going. And, it's inevitable, like the return to Earth for any infatuation. This doesn't mean that the society will fall apart. It just means that the reality of the society, the nuts and bolts, the grunt work, has to be done.

So the real question is '*now that we're in business as a society who is going to pay the bills?*' It is one thing to found a society, to get everyone excited. But, what about the day to day? And it's precisely at this junction that idealism and business clash. Idealism wants the spirit, while business wants the process. In the end, it's going to be process which wins. Process always wins because, at the end of the day, to survive requires practicality, not idealism.

The society's support comes from both the hard work of the founders as well as from sponsors' contributions. In every field, there are those who do the research and those who sell to those who do the research. The latter are vendors, suppliers, or go by some other title. It is the vendors who want to increase the business and become active supporters of the organization. They may join the organizing committee, con-tribute papers (a less frequent occurence), or support the meetings through monetary donations (increasingly the case). It's not all bad, however. There's absolutely nothing wrong with having organizations support the new society. It's a wonderful way for the society to be supported in its young years, allowing it the chance to grow, to remain vital, and to try new things.

The real problem comes when, over time, cliques form in the society which are al-lied with one supplier and against another one. These cliques can high jack the confer-ence, especially when their members get onto the organizing committees for meetings. Of course, in the professional world, one is presumed to value scientific validity and credibility above everything, but when the presenters are both scientists on the one hand and vendors of services on the other (also called solution providers), we have the makings of a festering corruption. Such corruption characterizes many societies that begin with ideals, but inter-mix solution providers with presenters and exhibitors in a way that blurs the line. None of us are able to resist such opportunities to promote our business, even when we blur the lines a bit ourselves.

How a professional society can remain vital

If *homo economicus* is destined to always rear its head and perhaps, in some measure, corrupt what it touches even without meaning to do so, then is there any hope? Or, are all professional organizations doomed to the slow change, from idealistic found-ers who cared a great deal about the field, those who maintain the society, and finally into the hands of a few individuals who use the society as a way of increasing their business?

If this question sounds totally out of place, we might want to look at the lessons of history. Greece was a democracy. Rome was a republic. Both were founded on the noblest of motives. Each civilization began with leaders who were above reproach. Popular leaders in Greece were occasionally banished for a period of ten years, per-haps because of their popularity and the fear that they might become tyrants. And, in the end, both civilizations suffered periods of oligarchy, of corruption, of rule of the few instead of rule for the many. Neither civilization nor, indeed, any civilization can escape the venality that comes with power and control. It's part of us, wired into our DNA. And professional societies, although hardly the likes of Greece and Rome, still allow these motives to play out. The ultimate result is a less than vital society, despite the fervently good hopes of the founders who themselves were idealists.

We ought to keep in mind here that we're talking about an organization which lives beyond the life of its founders, which comprises members of different abilities, where membership is voluntary, and where the ultimate aim of the society is to fulfill the needs and wants of the profession. Perhaps the most important thing for the society to do is to maintain intellectual openness and rigor. As we noted above, there is a tendency for governing bodies of organizations to get into a rut, into a way of 'doing things'. At first, these might be small things, such as having an unusual number of members who are somehow professionally related to each other; i.e., client and vendor, or groups of vendors who work together with a limited set of clients. That's not the bad part. It's an issue of 'birds of a feather flock together'. People with common interests will tend to join the organization.

The real problem, however, starts when people begin to realize that the society can control what is happening in the field. The society can begin selecting certain speakers, creating a small cadre of friends who nominate each other. It's done all the time, typically using the excuse that the people who are selected have been 'vetted'. Eventually, however, speaking engagements are closed to outsiders. A good solution for this is to have a competition with submitted papers, following a specific format. And, of course, there needs to be fair judging, perhaps totally blind judging. The bottom line here is that the society must consciously make the effort to include opinions and presenters other than those of the narrow clique who run it. Furthermore, these speakers must not be a simple 'bone' thrown to satisfy criticism, but must represent openness to new ideas. Otherwise, and inevitably, the organization will become a vehicle by which the organizing committees and the society management gain new clients for their own businesses. That is the seed of destruction.

✫ ✫ ✫

PART 3

PLAYING WITH OTHERS

CHAPTER 10

KEYS TO THE KINGDOM – PRACTICAL STEPS TO A MORAL LIFE

<u>Introduction</u>

The notion of morality is not particularly popular today in the early decades of the 21st century. We don't hear people talking about Cicero of Rome, Lord Acton of England, or about the principles of the Founding Fathers of the United States. We live in an era of moral relativism, where each group of individuals, each country, each civilization is accorded the undeserved privilege of being judged by its own norms. This multi-culturalism naturally spills over to the business world, to the world of the university, and to the world of research. And, how could it not do so? When men make rules, rules don't make men. There are no universals.

Having said that, what if we were to prescribe a moral life for the young researcher or the young employee? What are the words of advice to give the new person on the block, the just-minted Ph.D., the young hopeful starting a job, the slightly older professional working his (or her) way through a corporation and a career? Are there words of wisdom?

The answer is, of course, yes. And the wisdom is old wisdom, not new-age multi-culturalism, relativism, anything-goes, and the like. Indeed, when we've finished describing some of the facets of *'how to be a person'*, you may well think you're reading an ethical treatise. And, perhaps, you are. Perhaps this entire book is merely an updated, particularized version of ethical treatises of days gone by. That wouldn't be so bad either.

<u>Discipline – the first secret of success</u>

Discipline your desires and discipline your actions. Inevitably, you will be successful. It's not the grand vision which will bring success, letting you achieve what you want. It's the daily work, the small things, one atop the other, in endless succession, perhaps mind numbing, but nonetheless succession. Do things, period. With a bit of luck and intelligence, you will achieve what you want, if what you want is within reasonable range. Do things systematically, and you will achieve probably more than you ever wanted, more than you ever thought possible. You will have disciplined yourself.

<u>Moderation in everything – the second secret of success</u>

Everything in moderation is hardly a new concept. The Greeks and Romans talked about moderation. Aristotle recognized the middle to be the safest route. Do not do anything to excess, but at the same time, do not feel that you are free to avoid doing something. It's not reasonable to work to excess, even to succeed to excess. A moderate amount lets you enjoy the moment and its benefits, without forcing you to give up the pattern of your life to achieve the one goal. And, even charity should be given in moderation, else you become a ward of the state, and bring hardship to others.

Modesty and humility - the third secret of success

The world is not about *you*. Despite the fact that you live within yourself and cannot possibly know the true inside of another, the world does not revolve around *your* needs. Yes, you are the most important person to yourself. But just think, there are so many you's that if each person were to demand a separate set of values, nothing could proceed. So run after modesty. Make humility a constant companion. And, even when you become great, know that you do not create yourself. A higher power created you. So why be arrogant ? You did not create yourself; you are only the instrument of that higher power.

Courage, not foolhardiness – the fourth secret of success.

What is courage, really? It could be the momentary bravery shown in war, during the height of a pitched battle. Soldiers win medals for that. And, all too often, and so sadly, they die for their bravery. But we're not talking about the war that lasts a short time. We're rather talking of a different type of courage, the courage to keep to your vision, to confront the opposition, and not to give up. It's so very easy to stop when you are challenged, and the challenger clearly in the wrong. It's easy to yield to the group, abandon what you think is right. But in the end, you will lose the very essence of yourself. Now, as for foolhardiness, it's also not particularly wise to maintain a position that you, yourself, have come to realize is wrong. As George Bernard Shaw said:

Those who cannot change their mind cannot change anything.

And, as Oscar Wilde said:

Consistency is the last refuge of the unimaginative.

So, be courageous, not foolhardy, sticking mightily to what you believe to be right, yet ready always to change if that right proves to be a mistake. In so doing, you will have the wisdom of courage, and the blessing of honesty.

Taking stock of yourself

When all is said and done, know thyself. Socrates, through the tongue and pen of his student Plato, would say this again and again, teaching us that the greatest goal we might entertain is to know ourselves. That voyage within, where we pull from our depths that which is the essence of our soul, is the one voyage worth taking. So, learn about yourself with the same assiduousness that you master the subjects of arts and sciences. You, yourself, are also a worthy subject of study, especially in the years when you form yourself.

And yet, as you learn about yourself, you must be ready to change. In the words of Joseph Campbell:

> *We have to be willing to get rid of the life we've planned to have the life that is waiting for us.*

When honestly and respectfully taken, that voyage and its return makes us ready to be ourselves, ready to stand by what we believe, ready to entertain success with moral probity, ready with character that will stand us for a lifetime.

Kissing the hand of your teacher

Who is greater; one's parent or one's teacher? In Jewish ethics this question appears again and again. When parents and teacher come into the room, for whom does one truly stand? If there is insufficient food, whom does one feed? And at a march, whether wedding or funeral, or even academic march, who precedes whom in the place of honor?

Does it not say in the Ten Commandments '*Honor thy father and thy mother*'? Yet, practice among Jewish students is to stand for both parents and teacher, but for teacher first. And, in those simple actions, is yet another lesson. Your parents gave you life; your teacher lets you give yourself life. And, when all aspects are tallied up in the great scoreboard of life, it's the teacher's contribution that is seen to be the greater.

Summing up

These are the keys of the kingdom. You can read about them in any ethical treatise. Read Plato's Dialogues; they're there. Just open up Cicero and you'll get these principles. Open up the English philosophers, like John Stuart Mills, and you'll get the same thing. Open up Machiavelli and you'll get these same principles, not so much in the way they're presented here, but as starting points from which the ruler might wish to creatively diverge in search of power and control. So you, student, are yet another wanderer on the road to self-wisdom, just as all people who are earnest seekers after truth discover themselves to be. Take stock of yourself; that is the true journey, and the appropriate road upon which the student must travel.

✲ ✲ ✲

CHAPTER 11

KARMA, CHARACTER, AND THE LAW
OF 'WHAT GOES AROUND COMES AROUND'

<u>Introduction</u>

Beyond the topics of your research, and you yourself as a member of a research team, or even, heaven-forbid a non-researcher employee, lies your soul. That's right, your soul. We often think that we will go through life untempted, unscathed and unharmed. To be all those 'uns' is to be unconscious. The reality of our lives is so much different. We may want to do what's right, we may have been raised with strict morality, but life has a way of bending us, bending our paths, and bending, even distorting,, our moral compass. And so this chapter, which may not seem particularly appropriate in a book on your entry in professional adulthood, but needs to be written and read nonetheless.

<u>Karma</u>

We begin with the mystical notion of karma, which according to that fount of knowledge, Wikipedia®, is:

> *Karma (<u>Sanskrit</u>)....is the concept of "action" or "deed" in <u>Indian religions</u> understood as that which causes the entire cycle of <u>cause and effect</u> (i.e., the cycle called <u>samsāra</u>) originating in <u>ancient India</u> and treated in <u>Hindu</u>, <u>Jain</u>, <u>Sikh</u> and <u>Buddhist</u> philosophies. In these systems, the effects of all deeds are viewed as actively shaping past, present, and future experiences. The results or 'fruits' of actions are called karma-phala.*

Cutting right to the chase, the word *karma* summarizes it all. The key phrase is 'the effects of all deeds are viewed as actively shaping past, present, and future experiences'.

Now for the $64 question. What does all this have to do with one's business behavior? That's a good question. The answer is, as all those who have lived life know, 'everything'. You don't live in a vacuum. You live with people. What you do today when you are in power, have a job, have a chance to help others will come back to help you later or, perhaps, to haunt you. There is no escape; not really.

<u>Why character is so very important</u>

It's occasionally said, tongue in cheek, that character is what happens to you when no one is looking. We're all accustomed to being evaluated, and to putting on our best faces, putting on good shows for the judges, doing our best. But that's only for a very small part of our lives. What about the rest of the time, when the judges aren't looking, when we are free to be who we want? Who are we, and why should it matter? After all, don't we live in a world of *realpolitik*, where what's best for the state (or ourselves) is by definition 'good'? Don't we live in a business world that extols 'looking out for #1'? Aren't we citizens of a world where Sun Tzu and Machiavelli are the guides to success, where only the 'little people pay taxes' (courtesy of the late Leona Helmsley), and where, in the end, Gordon Gekko was right, 'greed is good'?

Of course, when you have a litany of such statements you recoil a bit. Or do you? Do you smile inside, wishing that you too could have the courage to be cruel, single-minded, a loyal follower of the bitch-goddess success?

If all of this annoys you, and you want to skip it, come to the other side, to where character and morality reign. The truth of the matter is that being decent is rewarding. It's fundamentally nobler. It gets you further, because it instills love in others for you, rather than fear and loathing. And, you get more from love than from fear. Finally, for the most part, you sleep better at night, at least if you are young. When you get older, it's harder to sleep at night, noble or not noble. But, at least if you're a noble soul, you get some of the benefits in your youth.

And, one last thing. Most books about business ethics emphasize acting in a morally upright way. It's the way we are constructed, despite statements to the converse. We instinctively smile when we see one person helping another, when a person in business is honest, when one can successfully resist temptation to crush one's opponents, instead sharing the goodies. We may cynically state that the kind, noble person who doesn't take everything for himself is a fool. But, if given a chance to be friends, we'd rather be friends with the fool than with the conquering, rapacious, successful businessman reputed to show no mercy.

Perhaps it's just that we're built to appreciate someone with a noble soul, despite the ever-presence of *homo economicus* that drives us all. Our mothers, who guided us, put that appreciation of nobility into us. It sticks there after all these years.

The golden rule

In your career, if you remember nothing else of a moral nature, keep the golden rule close to you and follow it. '*Do unto others as you would have them do unto you*' is an aphorism by which to live. It will take care of you in ways that you do not know, at times when you most need it. It will enrich your soul, leave you with few regrets and, in some cases, pile upon you riches of accomplishment and even money.

In the words of Richard Nelson, formerly research manager at the Campbell Soup Company, and an inveterate if a bit acerbic observer of company behavior, '*you don't always get what you pay for, but you don't get what you don't pay for'*. The golden rule is an investment strategy. In your career, in your business life, and even in your personal life, think about investing yourself. If there is an opportunity to help someone else, do it. It may be nothing to you and, indeed in the grand scheme of things, it may be irrelevant. Yet to the person who you help, in that specific minute, reaching out may make all the difference.

People in companies, in their careers, often live lives of quiet desperation. Companies can steal the souls from people, forcing people to act against their own nobler characters, driving out the softness that lubricates person-to-person interchanges. Careers are hard. And, long careers, decades long, are even harder, drying the soul, flaying the spirit, and sucking out the marrow of one's innards. It is in these moments that your act of kindness may become a lifesaver.

Of course, you may ask whether or not you will receive anything in return. In our lives we often use the economics metaphors, such as *'what will be my return on investment for this good deed'?'* And, in fact, you may not get anything from this individual, at least anything that you can directly trace to this act of kindness. It's not a tit-for-tat world. Yet a lifetime of observation suggests that there is some type of universal economy. These acts of goodness do come back, perhaps in ways that are not perceptibly linked to specific good deeds. Yet there are returns to these acts. And sometimes, in the quiet moments of meditation, you may 'feel' the connection between good things happening now and certain kind acts you did before. There may not be a clear visible connection, but there is a feeling that the connection exists.

And so, this is the golden rule. Do unto others as you would have them do unto you might be better phrased as *'Do unto others, for that will be done unto you'*. It's not a prescription, but rather a prediction, a statement of linkage, a flash of insight about how the world actually works, that world that we can feel but not necessarily see.

From this exposition of the subtle actions of the golden rule in business, let's move to a number of observations which are corollaries to this rule:

1. <u>Pay forward</u>. We've all heard of the notion of 'payback'. Generally payback is taken in its negative sense, as punishment for something bad that happened before, although payback can also be used in the positive sense. In either case, payback means that someone did something to another and that, later in time, that other person is returning in kind. Think about the notion of payback, but this time in the forward direction. Why not make an investment in the future by some favor, some good deed? It could mean inviting a colleague to be a co-investigator on a project and a co-author on the paper. Or it could mean sharing the leadership of a strategic initiative in a business effort. In either case, you are investing in the future. You're not paying back. You're creating a relationship

with the other individual based on your positive deed. You're putting money into an emotional bank, in the hopes that in later times you will be rewarded, either by the person to whom you are giving, or by someone else as the circle of good deeds gets bigger. It doesn't always work, but you'd be surprised how these small acts generate good feelings, and those good feelings, in turn, create positive futures for you. If you can invest in a saving account or in stocks, then you can invest in your future. A little of your professional capital today invested in this way will eventually earn dividends when you are systematic about these small, but meaningful, pay-forward investments.

2. Ignore slights. The old proverb continues to work today: '*to err is human, to forgive is divine*'. We're not talking here about being a saint. Rather, during the course of your career you will come up against many different situations where you may feel someone is slighting you. The truth of the matter is that you will be unduly sensitive in most of these situations. What you perceive to be a slight (i.e., your questions are ignored, you are not the center of attention, some of your best ideas are challenged) will be, no doubt, simply part of the give and take of a normal professional life. Don't waste your time being angry about a perceived abuse of your *amour propre*. More likely, the so-called abuse is either an oversight or the result of a different agenda on the part of the other person, an agenda which doesn't even include you. You can waste a lifetime feeling slighted, injured and abused. Don't waste the time. It's not coming back.

3. Never, never abuse the power you have been given. During the course of your career, you will often come into positions where you can exert control over other people. These are the moments that will try your soul. Be very careful about these moments. When you have power over people, such as supervising a subordinate or giving out contracts, there is the tendency in all of us to enjoy the feeling of power. In some cases, the boss may actually believe that he is superior, or the person having control of budgets to allocate to outside contractors may come to feel a sense of superiority to them. In such moments, you may make a terrible mistake, such as abusing those subordinate to you, or your suppliers. And that mistake could fester in the minds and memories of others. Even if you are not inclined to saintliness, try here. You don't want to be thought badly of by others over whom you had control. In the vernacular, '*what you do could come back to bite you in the ass*'.

4. On the other hand, the good you do may be buried with you – so don't stay up waiting for repayment. Although it's a good idea not to abuse power, being good may not do much for you, although it is a virtue, and something to be desired. You can sleep better at night. As Shakespeare had Mark Antony say in the famous lines from Julius Caesar:

"Friends, Romans, countrymen, lend me your ears. I come to bury Caesar, not to praise him. The evil that men do lives after them; The good is oft interred with their bones."

- *Act 3, Scene 2.*

When it comes time for the end, and we all must get there sooner or later, you won't be necessarily happy with your triumphs over people, and certainly won't be happy with the thought of those you may have destroyed on the way to the top. You will, however, be happy with the memory of the good you do, even if it ends up being yours privately, without anyone else knowing. Aim for good. It's the best way. At the end of the day, it's probably best to pursue the virtuous path, simply because it is right, and nothing more.

5. <u>The world didn't start with you, and it won't end with you either.</u> As you proceed in your life, keep in mind that you are only one person, with a finite lifetime behind you, and a finite number of years ahead of you. It's hard to realize that there will be others left after you're gone, and that you'll be a memory, lucky even to be remembered by your colleagues 10-20 years after your passing. Keep that in mind, and be modest. You are part of the world. And the world doesn't revolve around you. You'll realize the truth of this insight when you're about 60 years or older, and you see your colleagues dying. You get a sense of temporary sojourn on this planet. Enjoy that feeling; it's liberation from the agony of being self-important.

6. <u>There are other people, you know.</u> People are fundamentally interested in themselves. So, it should come as no surprise that when you talk about ME, when your conversation revolves around ME, when the contributions are MY achievements, that other people tune out. You may not perceive this tuning out, especially as you regale others about that most important person in the universe, YOU. It's pretty hard to get out of such a way of thinking. But you can. Try using the word "YOU" as much as you can in conversation. In addition, when other people talk, try nodding your head in agreement. At first, it will feel rather silly. But, over time, you will find that these motor actions, saying "YOU", nodding your head, will connect you with others, and will bring to a happy cessation this focus on ME. And, as an additional benefit, nodding your head back and forth is good for your neck and stops you from talking, letting you listen more.

7. <u>It's the small things that matter.</u> Very often we hear that you shouldn't 'sweat' the small things and that everything is, in essence, a small thing. This piece of

advice could be more correct than you believe. The truth of the matter is that just about everything you're going to do comprises a series of small things. Screw up the small things and soon the edifice of your life will crumble. This is especially true for your work. No, you don't have to be perfect in your work. But, you should try to make sure that your work is 'right'; that the small details are correct. There's a reason for this. People don't necessarily see the big picture. They don't see the goals or the grand scheme of things. And so, when people judge you, they evaluate you on what THEY can see. And those things — well, they're the small things. Misspell a word and you'll be judged harshly, not because you're a bad speller or lousy typist, but because (incorrectly) your basic ideas are weak or even incorrect. People see the small things and, in their mind, those small things are translated to judgments about your abilities. A piece of advice — use the spell checker on your computer. You'll be perceived to be a 'better' person, better researcher, even if it just ain't the case.

8. <u>Sharing the glory increases it more than you could ever realize.</u> You may feel that the world is horribly competitive, and it is. The famed Jewish sage, Rabbi Hanina, is reported to have said "*Pray for the welfare of the government, for if people did not defer to its authority, they would eat each other alive.*" With such a world view, it will do wonders for you and your career if you share the glory. Recognize that it's not you against the world. Hoarding the glory won't make you any safer. Sharing credit with others, inviting others to work with you on visible projects, publishing with others, and giving others the chance that they 'need' will go a long way. People don't forget kindnesses, not really. The good may be interred with you, but the truth of the matter is that if you are kind to a sufficiently large number of people, the kindness will be returned, somehow.

Summing up

At the end of the day, you will die. It's inevitable. Keep that in mind. And, as you plan your day, your year, your career, ask yourself about what you value most in your life. What would you like to be said at your funeral, written on your gravestone, talked about when people remember you? And, finally, choose the moral path. You will gain, your career will blossom, and the rewards to your soul will be incalculable. At the end of the day, you will be the person you were meant to be, and your career will be a fitting accompaniment and adornment for the life you will have led.

✪ ✪ ✪

CHAPTER 12

PLAYING WITH OTHERS WITH WHOM YOU WORK

Introduction

When you have a little spare time, go to the library and read the life histories of some famous scientists. Make sure that you don't read any of the very long, complete treatments of lives in science by writers whose efforts uncovered all the facts, interesting ones and just factoids. That's not going to serve the purpose of this chapter. Rather, read the popularized versions, such as *Microbe Hunters* by Paul de Kruif, an 'oldie but goodie'. What you want to do is a get a sense, a snapshot of the scientist in action, a feeling of what happened.

One impression you may walk away with is that the famous scientists who are written about, almost as heroes by some biographers, seem to be doing most of their work alone. Yes, there are assistants, associates and a network of collaborators and so forth, but the focus is on the lone scientist, working, fighting to uncover truth.

The truth of the matter is *that it ain't necessarily so*. The vast majority of science takes place in groups of individuals working together. The famous line '*no man (read also woman) is an island*' is never as true as it is in science. Today's science is a group affair, a mini eco-system, with one or two scientists at the top, the so-called principal investigators, but with an entire phalanx of other individuals providing support functions, consultation, and the like.

To get a sense of the collaborative nature of science, simply thumb through any of today's scientific and business journals. Many of the articles will be authored by groups of researchers, especially those that use technology, where the abilities of many individuals, not just one, are harnessed to do the experiment. There are, of course, still many one-person articles, often for the easier-to-execute experiments, or for theory papers where a group of collaborators is not necessary to do the actual work.

Let's now move forward to the unwritten rules of collaborating in groups. You may get a feeling of psycho-babble here, especially if you are a young researcher, ready to 'tear up the tracks, full of piss and vinegar'. Yet, a bit of wisdom at this time may pay out for years to come, as you learn to play with others in the environment of groups, where a lot of research is conducted. So, here goes.

Not playing with others is no longer an option

In our connected, increasingly complex world, no one can go it alone. The fable of the single, brilliant scientist is just that, a fable. Certainly, there are the eagles, the grand masters, the ones to whom the world kow-tows. But the truth of the matter is that these are very rare eagles. And, if you're reading this book, it's likely that you are not one of these eagles. You have to learn to play with others. It's the way the world works. You can be by yourself, but you'll need resources to do your work unless you are another Gauss or Einstein, and your laboratory is between your ears. Anything less and playing with others is a *sine qua non*, whether or not you recognize it.

At some point you will be the new kid on the block

Most of us who work in organizations learn the rules of the organization or, in the end, we're shown the door, either directly and bluntly or indirectly by being eased out under one pretext or another. We often know these hidden rules, even when we cannot articulate them. We adjust our behavior accordingly.

But what about the new kid on the block? We've all been the new kid, even if we began in the laboratory or research group or, in fact, any job. Our first days, weeks, even months on the job were marked by discomfort. When we were graduate students, we often morphed, generally subtly, from fun-loving college students without much responsibility to more frightened and aware graduate students. When we finished our degrees, we went for a post-doc (post-doctoral fellowship) or a job. As a post-doc in someone else's laboratory, we were again the new kid on the block, feeling comfortable only when we had mastered certain skills. Or, when we began our first job, we felt uncomfortable, perhaps for a day, a week or a month, until we learned what was expected of us, and what we needed to do.

All research groups and, in fact, all groups of people, have established ways in which they work. Research groups have a purpose, so it's important for you as a newbie to understand that purpose, and the unwritten rules. Is the purpose of the group to get grants to support itself? Or is the group funded, without worries, by some organization or 'sugar daddy' (horrible expression, but oh so true)? What does the head of the group want – to be the best in the field, to just survive or, perhaps, to find another job and move to the next rung?

When you are entering your job or post doc as a 'newly-minted' professional, more than likely you're not particularly cognizant of these different motivations. For many new professionals in their first jobs after earning their degrees, it's a relief to be working. If you're interested in developing a career, your focus is more on what you can accomplish and how fast, rather than on the dynamics of the organization that you are entering. Petty squabbles, motives for being in the organization, ways that the organization functions, are probably pretty far from your mind when you begin your job.

When, on the other hand, you enter the organization with experience under your belt, with a sense of how other organizations work, and with clearly defined goals, you're probably just as interested in the dynamics of the organization as you are in your own goals. It's not that you're professionally interested in how organizations work as much as you realize that to work within an organization you ought to know how it thinks, moves, acts, and reacts. It's just a matter of experience that changes you from focusing on you alone to focusing on you in an organization that can help you or hinder you.

<u>Discovering the corporate culture</u>
At some point in your new post doc or job, you're going to be invited to have lunch. There aren't any set rules. Most likely, you'll just be asked to join a group for lunch. In the early days of your job, it's important that you become a member of the crowd, of the group, if only to make sure that you understand the culture.

In these early days, it's also a good policy not to talk too much. You certainly want to be accepted for yourself, but a good way to do that is to listen to what others have to say, and add a little of your own point of view. Just not too much. You're not joining the group to impress them. You're there to be a member. It's OK to tell people what you've done, as long as it doesn't come across as a boast or a challenge. The last thing people want to feel is inadequate. It's OK to share with people your accomplishments, but not out of arrogance and out of false modesty. People detect that false modesty. And, if you've achieved a lot, it will come out. You don't have to broadcast it, but you shouldn't hide it either.

Becoming one of the group brings with it a number of benefits. For one, it makes work better. It isn't good to work alone when you are in a group or a company. People have a way of helping each other, of supporting each other, and being there. You may not realize it, but each person needs the group, and the group needs the person. You're part of the group, and it's important to you. You may not feel yourself to be at the center of the group, in which case you probably never will be. But, over time, the good feelings of others with whom you work will be a lot more precious and valuable than you might realize at the start.

So how do you discover the corporate culture? The answer is simple; your mother may have told you. Listen. And when you're finished listening, listen some more. G-d gave people two ears and one mouth. So, there.

But seriously, you ask," Is that all there is?" The reality is that you can't penetrate the culture of a corporation or research group. You have to be invited and the way to be invited is to show up. That's right, show up, be a part of the group, listen, and try to understand what's being talked about and why. Are people talking about the scientific issues being addressed? Or are they talking about the nature of the profession or the industry? On a more mundane level, are they talking about the people in the company or group? Or talking about others outside the group? Or does the discussion veer away from the problems, the profession, the situation, and on to other outside issues? Are the issues heavy or light, professional, thought provoking, or merely passing the time in pleasantries? And, most important, if you were to describe what's being talked about, say to your mother, what would you say in an unvarnished way? Are you happy with what you hear? Or do you merely tolerate it? Or, perhaps, as is often the case, do you feel that it is strange, a bit alienating, and you don't really feel like you fit in?

This isn't a self-help book about corporate cultures, crazy bosses, in-fighting, looking out for #1, listening with the third ear, or any of the topics which so intrigue readers. Nor is it about scientists in corporations, or about the classic novels of personal development, the so-called *bildungsroman* in German. Rather, it's simpler, more practical. The message is that there is a corporate culture, and that you as a professional scientist or researcher ought to know about that culture because, for better or worse, you're part of it.

Office politics

Along with the culture of an organization is the inevitable politics which emerge. There may be a mythical time in the organization when there was no office politics, when everything was wonderful. Perhaps this mythical time occurred in the early days of the organization, when times were tough, when the vision of one person guided everyone in the quest for survival.

When everyone is fighting to survive in a new organization, somehow that fight brings out the best in people. Everyone appears to cooperate, even those who, in subsequent months, will prove to be the least group-minded and cooperative. New organizations have a tendency to bring out the noble. But, alas, such nobility is short lived. Long remembered but, in reality, short lived like the Mayfly which spends months developing and then has one precious day of flitting around, only to die. Everyone remember the Mayfly, but few realize that this beautiful insect doesn't live very long, and if it were to live, what behavior would it begin to exhibit!

What next?

Now that you have sensed the corporate or group culture, what do you do? The answer is nothing. You're armed with knowledge about the group mores so you know more or less what is expected, the norms of behavior and, of course, what is off-limits.

The most important point about knowing the culture is realizing that, despite your self image, your *amour propre*, you have to fit in. It's not a question of losing yourself in the group, but rather of knowing what types of behaviors are expected. When the group has an informal, but nonetheless quite regular, Friday afternoon lunch in the cafeteria where they discuss all sorts of topics, mainly those dealing with professional issues, it's a good idea to be there. The whole idea is to become conscious of what's happening around you.

One example of this consciousness, or rather lack of it, was the Friday afternoon 'sherries' held in the Department of Social Relations (SocRel) at Harvard University in the 1960's. These sherries, hosted on the 14th floor of William James Hall, were open to all of the professional members who had offices in William James Hall, which meant students in experimental psychology (6-9th floors), clinical psychology, and sociology (rest of the building).

These sherries were designed to have people meet each other. And, in many ways, they were quite successful. They succeeded in binding together many of the researchers in the building, especially those in SocRel, and in psychology's Center for Cognitive Studies, run by Professors Jerome Bruner and George Miller.

Such formal social occasions, run on a regular basis, provided a very important venue for people to meet each other, people who might see each other in the computer center or in the library, but not know each other. In these sherries, and their counterparts, lay and still remain, opportunities to knit together the organization in a way which academic collaborations, common classes, and informal meetings in the building simply do not. Cherish them; they are valuable. They will become more valuable as you become increasingly cognizant of what's 'really happening' at the interpersonal level.

✫ ✫ ✫

CHAPTER 13

BECOMING AN AGENT OF
CHANGE – *REALPOLITIK* AND STRATEGIES

Introduction

Today's companies proclaim everywhere they can,that they are agents of change. Their announcements typically have something to do with the fact that the company welcomes evolution and supports movement towards the new and glorious future that awaits all forward-lookers. To back up their announcements, HR (the Human Resources Department) puts up posters in the corporate offices and laboratories welcoming change, announcing that they are at the forefront of welcoming the 'tomorrow' in which we all will certainly live in just a few years. Corporate management is happy with these somewhat bombastic messages. Hopefully, the public rewards the messaging with a more positive view of the company. Its share prices may increase a bit ,although share price is more likely to be affected by concrete news rather than by corporate persiflage.

But what is the truth of the matter? Are these corporations really agents of change? When you read about new movements such as *open innovation*, which welcomes ideas and contributions from everyone, can you really believe what you read? Certainly, there are clear corporate actions which can be interpreted as supporting this open innovation, this movement towards the future. But most important – what about YOU in this world of change?

What's good for the corporation is not necessarily good for you, and vice versa

You and the corporation are rather different.The corporation is a giant behemoth or, perhaps, not such a big one but still fairly large.The corporation does not act like a person, despite what you might feel after reading these motivational signs created for the public image and the stock market. The corporation moves ahead by the concerted will of top management and the ability of their employees to execute that will. You, on the other hand, are certainly not a behemoth.You move ahead by a momentary decision to push your life in one direction or another. And, you and the corporation experience different outcomes. When the corporation makes a mistake, it moves on eventually.When you make a mistake, your career can be damaged, often irreparably.

The practical outcome is simple. When you're a corporation you keep moving. Sometimes you make the right decision, sometimes you don't. But, for the most part, you survive. When you're a single individual, you make sure you make the right decisions, each time. YOU, personally, cannot afford to make the wrong decisions in the way a corporation can. YOU have neither the resources nor the time to recover from such an error.

How people react to the prospect of change and what that means to you

People don't really like change. It frightens them, moving them out of the so-called (and overly-used) 'zone of comfort' into a place whose rules they don't know, whose direction is unclear, and whose very existence calls into play those long-buried fears of childhood. Ask people whether they welcome change and, of course, they say 'yes'. What else could they answer? A 'no' is about as politically correct as denying apple pie and motherhood. Just look at their eyes, see them wincing, tightening around their lips. You'll get a different picture, a real one.

So, people don't want change. Maybe you don't want change, either. And, if you're close to retirement, your 'boodle' locked up safely in tax-free municipals, and like to play on the golf course as often as you can, maybe you can live with no change. After all, you're there, you've made it, why rock the boat? Let the young ones do it.

But, what happens when you are at the start of your career, or in the middle, when you see that continuing the way you, your research, your company have proceeded leads to an early death, whether of spirit, career, or both? Now, what do you do? We're not talking here of the young spirited buck, the newly-minted professional filled with *piss and vinegar*, prepared to ride off into the wilderness on the hero venture and return with new lands and infinite riches. No, we're talking here of young, competent professionals, who realize that to continue in the same way is to condemn themselves to a rather sad, even impoverished or, at the least, a not comfortable middle age and beyond. What are these ordinary, bright, perceptive professionals to do?

It is from that realization of the inevitable, coming inexorably down the road, lumbering slowly but unstoppably, that one knows that it is time to prepare to change and to prepare for change. And, thus, does adversity or its anticipation, make heroes of us.

So, now you see the ugly truth, that people don't like change. What, in fact, does this really mean to you, especially if you must embrace change to survive? Well:

1. You won't hear talk about the fear of change. Rather, you should expect to hear lots of talk about how change is desperately needed. There's a simple reason for this talk. No one wants to be identified as 'against change'. So, it's important to be 'seen' as being pro-change.

2. You will, however, get a sense that all is not right, that there is something in the way of change, but you can't quite put your finger on it. Your sense is probably

correct. People can block change while at the same time being perceived as pro-change. They can ask for many different 'bids' from suppliers to do a project, and spend their time comparing and contrasting these bids, studying every aspect of each bid. People can be busy with their current work, slowing down just enough so that nothing new can come in. Or, they can go to course after course, meeting after meeting, to deal with change, and 'hide' at these meetings. Companies love to send people for 'training', to enrich the job. Sometimes the enrichment can become a full time job, allowing the person to avoid making any decision at all!

3. When you are lucky enough to begin a new direction and produce some change, you'll hear pearls of wisdom such as *'we have to crawl before we walk'*, or some other such drivel. What you're really hearing is *'we have to stop this change or slow it down, so it doesn't overwhelm us and move us out of our comfortable, daily routine'*.

Ensuring that no one can really stop you

How do you start change in a world where everyone will say yes, but really mean 'no'? Perhaps the most frustrating part of wanting to change is the number of obstacles that are put in your way. Can you overcome these obstacles in a way that doesn't get you fired? What should you do, and how should you do it?

Start with the realization that *'it's better to ask for forgiveness than for permission'*. Or, as those in favor of citizens owning guns, *'I'd rather be tried by 12 of my fellow citizens than carried by 6'*. Both are saying the same thing; it's better to do than not to do, and not to trust in your fellow professional. As the psalmist says (Psalm 146, v 3):

Put not your trust in princes, nor in the son of man, in whom there is no help.

Now, for the good part, the 'what do you do'? Keep in mind that you are an agent of change in a world which doesn't want change. You certainly cannot convince each person, one by one, of the need of change. You don't have enough time or energy to 'arm-wrestle' each person and, besides, the old wisdom continues to hold: *'a man convinced against his will, is of the same opinion still'*. That last phrase, by the way, is from Dale Carnegie's book *How to Win Friends and Influence People*, in the chapter "*You can't win an argument*".

So, you have to do something else. The something else should be feasible, scalable and, most of all, so clear, so obvious, so impactful that anyone going against it will come out looking like a fool. You don't want to take any prisoners on this one.

The unstoppable strategy: Small-scale studies to demonstrate your point

When you begin a new area of research, the prudent thing to do is a pilot study. The pilot study usually flies *'below the radar'*, so you have space to try out ideas. If the pilot fails, then you are at once wiser, as well as a bit sadder. Most new researchers don't really know whether their research 'will work'; so this pilot study is a valuable first step.

Since pilot studies are real, why not use the pilot studies when you are dealing with people who may or may not want to change? You really can't get into their minds, so the truth of the matter is that no matter what other people say, you probably should take what they say with a grain of salt. You don't know whether they are telling the truth, being polite, being politically correct, or as all too often happens, waiting for you to trip up, and then apply the coup de grace to you.

A pilot study, undertaken when you are trying to convince other people, makes a great deal of sense. For one, you learn about the 'what' that you are preaching. This means that you can 'talk the talk' and 'walk the walk'. You have experience in the area. Of course, the pilot study is small by definition, but it is a real study, rather than simulated data. So, what you will talk about will, by your own efforts, have the 'ring of truth'. You've done it; you set up the study, and collected the data. What you present is real; your audience will sense that. They will believe you more readily because people believe data and experience. It's hard to politely 'blow you off' or dismiss you when you come with data. (Of course, behind your back those same polite individuals may proceed to stab you to death, but you cannot control that).

WAVE 0 - How pilot studies sell in IdeaMap.net During the past decade, experimental design of ideas, i.e., conjoint measurement, has become an accepted tool in consumer research for the evaluation and optimization of concepts. Yet, most prospective clients pay mere lip service to the approach, but in practice choose to commission focus group sessions, or evaluative tests of single test concepts.

When conjoint measurement was very expensive, selling the approach required many meetings with clients in what ended amounting to an education. The process was painful and, more often than not, both frustrating and unproductive. And so, clients were able to get away with their delaying tactics. After all, no one could complain because the client was guarding corporate monies, doing the prudent thing. Such were the conditions that nurtured inaction, client inertia, and the wonderful world of the decision 'NO'.

When we developed IdeaMap®.net in the late 1990's and early 2000's, we realized that we might well go bankrupt were we to 'arm-wrestle' every client to get them to use the program. It was one thing to spend a lot of time educating clients on how to do experiments and use programs when the price tag was upwards of $35,000. It was something quite different to get clients to *use a program or work on a project with us when the price tag was a third as much, around $12,000. There was simply not enough money to fight the fight. It might take four or five exposures to a client and, in the end, the projects were not sufficiently large.*

It was then that we realized the value of a pilot study. Rather than spending the all-too-often unproductive three-five visits to convince the client, we offered to do a small study, virtually at cost, to demonstrate the value of our approach. We knew that we could do the study quickly, virtually overnight, and that all we had to do was show the results in order to sell the client or, in some less than pleasant situations, kiss the client goodbye.

This approach became our 'Wave 0', christened so by colleague Steve Onufrey. We offered to do a small project, in two days, if the client would pay the field cost for no more than 50 people (i.e., respondents). We insisted on limiting the number of respondents to 50 so that the client could not do the study for 'free', under the guise that the client wanted to see the approach demonstrated.

To cut to the chase, the Wave 0 strategy worked then and still works today. Clients serious about working with the approach will accept the challenge of a Wave 0 project. And, when they see the results, they realize that the research method can help them. Why? Because they see it with their own data! Prospects who hem and haw, who can't find the time, are summarily discarded. They, in fact, really don't want to proceed. So, why waste time? On to the next.

Communicate your results – it's not about YOU, it's about THEM or IT

Listen to any conversation about new ideas. Not at a university, where they cherish new ideas, or ought to. (Actually the literature is filled with same-old, same-old, so don't listen too closely). Rather, listen to a conversation in a company. Don't bother reading the stuff that companies put on the wall, the HR blather about *innovation is our friend*, and so forth. Just listen to people in the company. You'll learn a lot, especially how people react to new ideas. Keep that in mind.

When it comes time to communicate your results, remember that you will be bringing in a new idea. And, remember that no one likes change; no one really likes new ideas. Oh, there may be one or two individuals who you meet, such as the president of the company, who welcomes new ideas. It's their bonus, their payout, their boodle. But, for the rank and file of corporate employees, *new* means discomfort, fear and it means rejection. The rejection can be just as easily brutal as it can be delivered by an iron fist in a velvet glove. Pioneers, those who are first, get the arrows in their backs. You're not on the leading edge, you're on the bleeding edge. And so forth.

So, now that you're either giggling, or a bit nervous, having 'there there, done that', what do you do? And, what do you do if you have to communicate new things to colleagues who don't care about 'new', 'better'?

<u>Simple is good</u>: Whether you are a graduate student, a young professional in a company, a newly minted Ph.D. post-doc or assistant professor, or even a wizened, battle-tested professional, simple is good. That's all. Simple is good. Don't baffle them with bullsh*t. That phrase, *'when you don't know, baffle them with bullsh*t'* doesn't hold. Your colleagues, clients, employers aren't sitting around waiting for you to confuse them. If you're not able to communicate your point simply, then you're already in trouble. Your audience won't respect you, either now or in the morning. And, your audience comprises people, just like you, who have very little love in their hearts. So, to reiterate the point, simple is good. In fact, simple is great. Oh, and beyond simple, *simple + clear* can't be beat.

<u>People do understand numbers</u>: After I had been in business a few years, it became increasingly clear to me that people are, for the most part, not particularly well-grounded in science. My colleagues in business kept telling me to 'dumb down' my presentations because the clients did not understand numbers. It was no good showing data. It was better to talk and talk and talk. They called it 'presenting the results to marketing in the way (they thought) marketing understands'. And, guess what? Those verbal presentations, sans numbers, were unbearably dull, abject failures! They were so boring that it was hard to stay awake writing them. It wasn't that the clients were unable to understand numbers. Rubbish; the clients loved the numbers! However, the numbers had to be presented in simple, cogent, clear ways that would immediately address the question. In fact, after one particularly unpleasant, text-only presentation 'choreographed' by a client named Winston (first name only), I called such text-only presentations 'Winstonizing' in his honor. I then swore that I would never again Winstonize a presentation. The only saving grace of that particular experience was the one table I snuck in, at the end, because I, myself, couldn't bear the presentation. Just too many words. The bottom line here – use numbers, but make the numbers simple and meaningful. Add some context. Then, you'll see the audience's eyes glue on the numbers. It works every time; try it.

<u>Don't drone</u>: You may be nervous. Try not to say 'uh huh' more than once in the entire presentation. If you're at a loss for words, just stop for a second. That momentary stop has greater impact than 'uh huh'. In fact, go to hear a presentation where the hapless presenter says 'uh huh'. At some point, you'll either be annoyed or you will start counting the number of 'uh huh's' to keep your attention.

<u>A short presentation is better than a long presentation</u>: The old saw works here – I would have made a shorter presentation had I more time to prepare. You may be enamored of your own voice, the wisdom of your efforts. You may think that unless you

pack your presentation with everything and take an extra 20 minutes to be 'complete', that you're failing. *Well, it ain't so.* Your audience has a limited, very limited, attention span. Short is good. Short and powerful is better. Short, powerful and clear is best. Most of all, short, short, short. If you can say it in 10 minutes, why take 15 minutes? Unless, of course, you want to ensure that no other actors have a chance to audition in front of your audience. Then, and only then, it's perfectly OK.

Don't patronize (talk down to your audience): Remember that your presentation sends a message about you and about your topic. Don't make the audience feel inconsequential. They may pay your salary, and they may determine your future. Many of us pontificate, either because we feel that we are superior (not true), or we really feel inferior, and patronizing others is a defense against our feelings of fear and inadequacy. The truth is, audiences sense the speaker's feelings. Audiences don't mind a nervous speaker. At least most don't, unless we're talking about something the audience is paying for, i.e. such as entertainment. And, if you're nervous, show it a little. The audience will be sympathetic. But, by all means, don't go in the opposite direction, talking down to people just because that allays your anxiety. You'll be sorry.

Summing up

If you're going to change the world, here's to you. But remember, changing the world isn't the same thing as getting straight A's on examinations, doing extra credit homework and, of course ,actively participating in class. The truth of the matter is that those skills may count in closed-end systems, in scholastic paradises, where adherence to the rules and slavish obeisance to norms really counts. No, you're in a new world, now, Toto. It's not Kansas anymore (nod to *The Wizard of Oz* and to Judy Garland's wonderful performance).

So, what do you do to change the world? Well, in the world of science, of academe, of knowledge workers in business, sheer effort doesn't matter. It's brainpower. You have to seduce the audience, win them over, put forth your ideas cogently. You don't score points for bullsh*t. Don't baffle your audience, convince them.

And how do you convince them? Well, the bottom line is data. But ,it's not just data;anyone can give data. The world is awash in data. Data are cheap. No, the answer is cogent data, that wakes up your audience, rouses them from their dogmatic slumber. Little studies, data that will shock them, but intrigue them; that's the way to do it. Not just relevant data, but data guaranteed to seduce, scare, delight and, ultimately, convince.

And if that's not enough, data with numbers. Not just interpretation. Data with numbers that tell the story, that hit the audience square in the eye. Data which poke at them a little. Data which makes them jut a bit more afraid. It's better to be feared after knowing your data, than to be happy after knowing your data. You want to change the world. The world doesn't get changed by happy campers. The world gets changed by hungry, somewhat (but not too) fearful people, by the hungry Cassius, with a look of hope, and a look of ambition. Seek these when you present your results; make your presentation simple and cogent. And, who knows, you may be well on your way!

✵ ✵ ✵

CHAPTER 14

BOO HOO – MY BOSS (PROFESSOR, COLLEAGUE, POST-DOC) DOESN'T LIKE ME

<u>Introduction – so what else is new, let's go for lunch</u>

Let's see, now. First, you're in elementary school or even kindergarten. Your teacher watches carefully for any sociopathic behavior, such as one child mercilessly hitting another. By the time you've finished kindergarten and elementary school, you pretty well know that some people are nice, others are just plain rotten and, of course, you're more towards the side of nice. High school is more of the same, only more subtle. Instead of outward displays of hostility, you'll encounter structured hostility, disguised as simple 'feedback' or 'comments' on yourself, but administered with the deftness of a surgeon's practiced hand.

And, of course, by the time you get through college and graduate school, you'll have recognized the world for what it is – a true incarnation of the blooming, buzzing confusion of William James, with the black tonality of Hobbes' life of man – nasty, brutish and short.

So, that should prepare you for your career. The point of this chapter is to talk about what to do when you get into your career, and find out that it's not all sweetness and light. We're not talking about the boss-worker relationship, about the 'craziness' of the workplace, about the vicious and cruel behaviors which manifest themselves there in full bloom, often of an institutionalized psychosis. Those are best taken up by other authors, whose psychological insights can bring a measure of relief to the hapless victim. No, we're going to talk about a different situation. We're going to talk about the hostility you may and, in fact, probably most definitely encounter, in the professional circles in which you currently or will travel. That hostility is much more relevant, far more interesting, and juicy, like a well cooked, well seasoned hamburger about to be devoured.

So let's go to it.

<u>You may be crazy, but there are people out to get you – so outlive them</u>

Just because you think that people don't like you doesn't mean you're seeing or imagining things. If truth be known, we live in a massively competitive world. Yes, you are taught in Sunday School or, perhaps instructed by your beloved nursery school or kindergarten teachers, that we all have to be friendly with each other. Perhaps you are a flower child, an airhead, who, with brilliant mind and good heart, managed to get through graduate school with an advanced degree.

That's all wonderful. But the truth of the matter is that in professional life many people believe that it's a so-called 'zero-sum game'. That is, if you get something, then someone else feels deprived. And so, every one of your achievements may well come at the perhaps ill-deserved, but, nonetheless, very real feeling, that someone else has been hard done by. That's why reviews are blind; it gives a chance for the hostile feelings to be expressed under the cover of professionalism.

So what do you do? Should you just ignore it? Should you try to get back at the person? Should you move on to somewhere else? All of the above? None of the above?

The answer is .. that there is no answer. You just have to live through it. The anger, mutual jealousy, mutual sniping may come to an end. One of you may move to another job, another university. Or die. Worse things could happen than outliving your enemies. Indeed, it was the late Dr. Boring, *eminence gris* of Harvard University's Department of Psychology, and major historian of the early days of experimental psychology, who opined '*You don't convince your enemies, you outlive them*'. And it was Boring who dutifully wrote the necrologies of his colleagues, perhaps with something more than simple sadness on his face when he was writing them. Boring lived to the ripe age of 81, dying in 1966. He outlived most of his contemporaries and also most of his enemies.

Dealing with it all when you're a helpless graduate student
Whenever I go back to Harvard, visiting my psychology department, I am increasingly struck by the apparent warmth, where there is actually an office devoted to increasing student morale. It's a sort of student ombudsman. I'm jealous. It seems like a warm, caring atmosphere. Sort of like the Joan Baez and Miriam Makeba kumbayah period; everyone sitting together, letting the love hang out.

It wasn't always so. Harvard's viewpoint, if one could apply that human term to an institution was '*every tub on its own legs*'. This famous aphorism meant that '*you're on your own*', whether the YOU was a department such as the psychology department, a research team or, ultimately, the individual graduate student.

Needless to say, this type of 'swim or sink' mentality bred a lot of depression, anger and paranoid behavior in the graduate students who were subjected to it. Sadly, there was no sense of comradeship. Students did not naturally ally with each other in an attempt to finish their work. Students were divided and afraid; not exactly the best breeding grounds for friendship and cooperation.

And so, there was the natural anger of students against each other, but rarely against the university or faculty. The question was not simply 'how to manage this anger', how to deal with it, but how not to let the situation demoralize everyone.

In such situations, students turned inward, away from each other. The sense of isolation was palpable. The fear was general, rampant, universal. But, in turn, it was good training. One learned to control one's fear, one's anger. It was good practice for the future. Those who were able to control their anger and outrage survived. Perhaps they were depressed, but they survived, nonetheless.

What's the lesson for us? The world you will face is not warm, kumbayah, let's all be friends. You're going into a world of competition, of egos, of unexpressed anger which, no doubt, you will experience in one or another manifestation. The strategy is simple. Keep your eye on the goal. It's not worth delving into yourself at this early time. No one cares. Not really. Although, perhaps your mother does.

In the end, you're on a journey. Don't let the situation, the competitiveness, the anger of others, or even the structure of dark fearsome places in the university hold you back. Move forward. Keep your eye on the goal; only on the goal.

Now what if you're just starting out in your career?
Outliving your enemies sounds like a great strategy if you're an old geezer (or geezerette). But what if you are young, just starting out in your job and, in total innocence, you run across a colleague who you describe as a 'rat', or some other loathsome creature? It's probably going to be a long time until one of you two die. And you've not even started your career! What bad luck; just at the start you're saddled with someone who you wish were dead, for whatever probably perfectly good reason you might have.

So what should you do? Is it worthwhile to conduct a guerrilla war? After all, if both of you are reasonably healthy, have few other job opportunities, and the money is good, you could well stay at the same job for years, jostling each other, sniping when convenient. It's a colossal waste of energy and it's bound to demoralize you. In fact, it could very well change you from a bright young thing to an embittered, *farbissene* (a wonderful Yiddish word), unpleasant-to-be-with professional. So long-term, guerrilla warfare doesn't work, unless you have no other talents, and feel that the war gives you a *raison d'etre, a reason to be,* that you would otherwise lack. What a waste of the precious few minutes of your life! Don't just fight; you won't win. If you do, it will be a joyless pyrrhic victory.

Go to Plan B. And what is Plan B? The answer is – whatever you want it to be, only executed with a positive end in mind for both of you. Perhaps, you just confront your nemesis, openly. It's best to do it over lunch. Or perhaps, you join forces, suggesting to your nemesis that you work together on a project. YOU choose the project and bring it as a gift offering. You don't have to debase yourself. Just discuss this joint project as if it were the most natural thing to do. Or, perhaps even more effectively, as you are discussing the project, ask your nemesis to do you some small favors, such as bring you something. People end up loving others, not for what they get from the others, but rather for what they give to the others. So, let your nemesis do something for you. Don't be proud; that would be stupid. Accept; that's being smart.

Life in early-mid career

By the time you have been in your career about 5+ years, you will begin to realize that the world is not a love-fest, filled with warm streams, rivulets, or even droplets of caring kindness. Rather, when you are on the track to publishing your work, you'll find that reviewers may not like you, that your experiments don't always work, and that you find yourself in competition with other people. By early mid-career, you're finished with the job of 'proving' yourself, and on to the job of 'establishing' yourself.

If you are just the tiny bit perceptive, you'll notice that some things have changed. Whereas before you were under the thumb of your professor, and you had to pass hurdles, whether examinations or your thesis as supervised by your committee, now you're somewhere else. The *somewhere else* is characterized by the following:

1. You don't have anyone checking on your performance, except yourself. Of course, people are looking at your performance, but you don't have 'tests' from the outside, rules, milestones that you have to obey.

2. Yet, you are somehow responsible for yourself. You're treated as an adult, i.e., with indifference. If you succeed, then that's fine. If you fail, well, that's ok also. You don't have a guidance counselor to tell you what to do.

3. You've already submitted the paperwork for a grant. You may have been accepted or, more likely, turned down. You're not innocent anymore. You know the pain of defeat. And, when you succeed and get your grant, you have a sense of a short term, but not a long term, guarantee. You'll live to fight another day. And you know quite well that you will have to fight.

Now that you've proven yourself and are establishing yourself, what should you do when roadblocks present themselves? And they surely will. Unless, of course, sometime in the early years of your career you found yourself drifting towards a state of nothingness, where you did nothing, came to expect nothing, and shrivelled up into the nothing which presages death. There are many who do so, out of a mistaken sense that it's better not to suffer than to strive and suffer. What a horrible fate to choose for oneself! The great English poet Alfred Lord Tennyson got it right in his 1842 poem, Ulysses. Poets often do:

It may be that the gulfs will wash us down:
It may be we shall touch the Happy Isles,
And see the great Achilles, whom we knew.
Tho' much is taken, much abides; and tho'
We are not now that strength which in old days
Moved earth and heaven; that which we are, we are;
One equal temper of heroic hearts,
Made weak by time and fate, but strong in will
To strive, to seek, to find, and not to yield.

But just because Tennyson got it right, and giving up could be a horrid fate, does not answer the practical question: what? What should you do in these early mid-career days, when you're not a newly minted scientist, when the bloom has somewhat left the rose (well, just a little anyway), when you have a life stretching out ahead of you and, of course, when you are taking on obligations. What should you do when, boom, the blockage hits you? You are stopped, stymied, shunted aside. Perhaps, all of them.

Well, first, *never, never, never give up.*

Now that giving up is out of the way, the next step is to look around rationally and make a decision. Is the blockage temporary? Is the blockage due to a situation that will rectify itself, i.e., funding is low for the current year and you cannot get any research monies? Or is the blockage more profound, say an enemy in the same department who you feel will fight to the death, or so it seems, to impede you? (It's probably not true. You may think the person's sole objective is to block you. People have more important things to do, other agendas, than to maliciously plot your demise. You're really not that important, you know, or should know.)

Perhaps the best thing to do is to deal with, and thus neutralize, the source of blockage. Again, when the blockage is a person, offer to collaborate. Bring 'something to the party', a nifty research idea, and opportunity. That will often ameliorate things. If that doesn't work because the problem is structural, such as only one position but two people vying, don't waste precious moments trying to beat the other person. If you win in that contest, fine. If you lose, you haven't built a survival strategy. Focus on surviving. Focus on other opportunities, in other places, whether 'other' be different sources of funding, or even a different job. Winning doesn't have to be everything if you end up dying in the conflict.

Life in later career

What's it like when you have braved the world for years? Do you reach some place where peace reigns, where your anxieties fall away like the isolated snowflakes of an early snow shower? Or is it more of the same, more hustle, more fighting, more holding your own in a world increasingly full of both friends and enemies?

Well, it's both. Later on in your career, when you have survived into middle age and older, things become more peaceful. The tempest abates a little, or at least problems, frustrations and troubles become more tractable, less irritating as you let them. Most of your early fights, your ambitions, your frustrations, inevitably fade. Some, of course, don't, but a lot of what you strived for years before will seem to be simply less meaningful. The anxieties that you had about establishing yourself have either driven you to succeed or didn't help you for whatever reason, and so you failed. In either case, many of those anxieties are long gone.

And so where are you? Well, for one, there are those 'enemies'. Many enemies over your career, or better phrased, many people who were obstacles, have moved on. They no longer affect you. Some have really moved on, to the next world. Your emotions, in turn, have damped. It's hard in later career to be as excited as in earlier career. You don't stay up all night talking science and future with colleagues. In fact, you find that it's even hard to stay awake when you talk to your colleagues. What was a delightful joust, a proving of your own mettle at the start, now has become yet another conversation, generally with a younger person trying to prove his mettle with you. *Plus qui change, plus qui rest la meme* (The more things change, the more they remain the same).

More things change as you enter mid career and, especially, later career. Those of you who have gone to conferences may well recall your excitement at these early conferences. If the conference was academic, then perhaps you remember the feelings of talking hour after hour, comparing notes, measuring yourself against colleagues who you might see once or twice a year, or even who you might meet once and never again. What heady days, to think of the challenges ahead of you! You got inspiration from these chats. And, when you were lucky enough to catch the attention of a senior eminence in the field, have your photograph with that person, chat for a few moments, and get the knowing nod, that was blessing enough, and you were happy.

Fast forward decades, to the same conference. Only this time, you are in mid late career and have been successful. No longer the young 'thing', it's now you who are assaulted by waves of younger professionals, seeking your blessing, your nod, your assent to work that they will describe to you *ad infinitum* and, in fact, *ad nauseum* if you just let them. And, beyond that are your colleagues, now friends, about your age or a bit younger, who have students they bring to these conferences. You are to bless these students, to give them inspiration, to guide them. But, your older friends, your mentors, those who blessed you? They're no longer here. Many of them are dead.

In the end, at mid and later life, you change. Or at least most people change. The energy, the vision may still be there. But the conversation changes, from what will happen in the future to shared memories of the past. You may do new work, but you find yourself thinking in a more historical way. It's memory now. You don't ask the 'what' about your new research as much as 'where does it fit in the history of the field?'

Your focus is on history, on place, on meaning, on motives of what you do as much as on the topic itself, and how you will benefit. In a sense, you are an adult now. You see where you belong, what you contributed, where it all fits. Wisdom comes to you, but first wisdom must chase out ambition. And wisdom almost always does in later career, when you realize that your net present value is 0. John Maynard Keyne's aphorism now becomes all too strikingly real; *'in the long run we're all dead'*.

Remember to look at the big picture

The old adage is that revenge is best tasted 'cold'. The better adage is that putting people in your debt early in the game is better than extracting revenge later on. Instead of looking at the world as a continuing joust, where you the gladiator just want to survive another day, think about the world as a place where people 'do' for each other. Make people want to 'do *for* you', not 'do *to* you'.

When you get a reputation for professional kindness, for doing favors, the odds are that things will go well for you, at least on the average, anyway. No, you won't be able to avoid all of the problems of life. None of us can. But, having people in your debt means that you have some allies. These may not be allies that you would guess today. Some of your best friends may do absolutely nothing for you, even though you have done many things for them. But there will be others, who, being slightly in your debt, will replay that small debt with far more. You don't know which of your colleagues, which people to whom you have extended kindness during you career, will return the gift of friendship, but there is bound to be one, two, or even more.

So the best strategy: pay forward, do things for people. Do things and don't expect anything in return. Cast your bread on the waters, and hope to heaven that you never have to swim in those waters. But if you do, casting enough bread honestly in the good times will come back as a help and a blessing in the bad times.

Summing up

Life isn't fair, life isn't necessarily fun. You're going to have enemies throughout your career. Some will be active, some will be passive. Those who are close to you may well be indifferent to you.

And, the answer to all this? Simply don't give up, but rather move forward. And, just as important, do favors for people, for many people. There will be times when you are on top. Use these times wisely to gather friends, to create emotional and real debts to you. For there will be other times when you are no longer on top, when more things seem bleak than you think you can ever tolerate. It will be at those times when you will be happily surprised, the payback from the good deeds you have done, and the kindness to others that you have shown.

✲ ✲ ✲

CHAPTER 15

PLAYING TOGETHER VERSUS COMPETING:
A STORY OF TWO CORPORATE FUNCTIONS

Introduction

Once you have finished your training and begin your career, it's important to learn how to work with your colleagues, those who support you, both inside and outside the corporation.   No professional employee is an island unto himself anymore. All people in companies are members of an ecology. No, it doesn't sound particularly romantic or professional, but the truth of the matter is that we cannot do everything ourselves. We depend vitally on others to get what we need done.

But what's the practical lesson here? All of us, more or less, know that we rely on others. Few of us could create our own computer, or write our own Windows® operating system from scratch. We know when it's in our interest to 'make something' from scratch versus when we should buy it 'off the shelf'. It's obvious for equipment, computer programs (unless one's ego is tied up in the program), for building services, and so forth.

However, it's not so obvious when the 'make versus buy' decision comes to professional services, where many of us are employed. With this lack of clarity in mind, let's investigate one specific area of a business, consumer-based evaluations of products, to see what type of life lessons we can learn.

The goal of this chapter is that you understand how the two groups do their jobs, how the individuals in both groups interact with external resources, and where each of these groups has 'gone' in terms of corporate position. You'll start to get a sense of the different behaviors in a corporation, and what might be the ultimate impact on your career.

The reason for choosing these two specific groups or functions is simply because I am intimately familiar with each. But, the truth is, that's not all. Each group possesses its own heritage, follows its own practices, and attracts different types of people. Understand how these two groups differ and you will understand the nature of conflict and cooperation in the corporation.

Corporate functions in the same 'space' – sensory analysis and marketing research

If you ever have a chance to walk the halls of a corporation, make it your business to go to two different groups. The first is the market research group and the second is the sensory analysis group. You'll find these groups primarily in the world of foods and beverages, in flavor and fragrance supply houses and, to some degree, in personal products companies. These groups may have different names such as consumer insights instead of market research, product guidance instead of sensory analysis. You'll figure out which group is which or you can simply ask someone in the business world who is conversant with the product area to tell you which group is which.

Both of these groups have the corporate-defined responsibility for 'understanding the consumer'. Both of these groups learn to understand consumers by testing them. A deep understanding of how they differ, the dynamics of corporate behaviors that each one follows, as well as the 'games that people play' is an education unto itself. This education will pay dividends over the years to come.

Let's begin a bit of history. It will show you how these groups evolved and how you, yourself, might want to guide your own evolution.

Sensory analysis and how it grew

It's a fact that a food or beverage that doesn't taste good, a cosmetic that doesn't 'work', a car that's not comfortable, will not sell well. Customers may at first buy, but sensory pleasure is important for their continued satisfaction. What was cute, interesting, low calorie, revolutionary, attention-getting the first time you consumed it or experienced it can become boring, painful, and downright unpleasant on repeated experience. And, in a demand-driven economy, where there is more than enough of everything all the time, sensory satisfaction is critical. Be unpleasant, become boring, fail to live up to expectations, and if you are selling a product that can be easily 'switched out', 'substituted', 'dumped, then you're yesterday's news.

Keep in mind that companies recognize that their products have to pass muster. It's not just enough for them to tell the consumer how wonderful the product is. That doesn't work, not any more. So, for the past seventy or so years, since around 1940, companies have invested in specialists who can guide product development, so that the product is acceptable, tastes good, looks good, and doesn't get tossed after being opened. The specialists who work with product developers go by a variety of different titles, depending upon the day's political climate, what's in, what seems to elevate their position. You'll know them as sensory analysts, sensory professionals, sensory specialists, product guidance specialists, and so on and so forth. You get the idea; they are involved in developing the sensory characteristics of the product. They work with appearance, taste, smell, touch, and hearing.

The specific work of sensory analysts might interest us, as it is filled with fascinating byways and stories. The history of sensory analysis in business, its role in the field, and the nature of how the sensory professional evolved is important knowledge for the young professional casting about, looking at the future. It teaches some very important lessons. We'll follow them in numbered format, allowing us to compare the same type of history to that enjoyed by market research, its corporate 'doppelganger', nemesis, and alter ego, all wrapped up into one.

1. <u>A practice, emerging without a systematized body of scientific knowledge</u>: Sensory analysis arose from the need to understand the sensory characteristics of products. Seventy years ago, no one was particularly expert in the sensory characterization of food. You might read about a chemist or product developer who 'got interested' in characterizing a product on which the person was working, then did some experiments, and eventually published the results in the scientific literature. It makes interesting reading. Here is a professional expertise in the development stage. The key thing to keep in mind is that the individual who performed the sensory analysis was a scientist, expected to be the expert. The person was not a businessman, i.e., marketer. And that will make all the difference as we move along in our story.

2. <u>Demand that the practitioner be facile in statistics, in a world where statistics savvy was rare, and computational power almost entirely absent</u>: Sensory analysis naturally made use of statistics. If you read the early literature scattered around, you'll find that the sensory analysis of the 1930's – 1950's relied very heavily on inferential statistics (i.e., does Product X different significantly from Product Y). Sensory analysts, therefore, became adept statisticians, something that was not the case for other people in the company. So we now have the first two foundation stones; sensory analysis as a 'self-taught' domain without any science (i.e., more like clinical practice than science), and sensory analysis as statistics-heavy.

3. <u>Skunkworks mentality</u>. Throughout the 1940's and onwards, sensory analysis adopted a skunk-works mind-set. The most important thing was to be able to do the study, from start to finish. Given the history of sensory analysis, the skunk-works mindset was understandable. First, sensory analysis did not arise as a corporate mandate seeking 'best practices'. There were no case studies in business schools dignifying the field. Second, people were accustomed to doing everything themselves. They were scientists, not business people. Scientists are accustomed to being self sufficient. Third, there was never much of a budget because their efforts were perceived as home grown, under-the-radar studies. And so, the skunk-works mentality took hold, first in the 1940's, and then later in the ensuing decades. Even when sensory analysis became a respected discipline, the skunk-works mentality remained. The 'we can do it all' mentality didn't go away.

4. <u>Need for self-esteem by becoming the low-cost supplier, rather than the value-add supplier.</u> The final evolutionary step occurred with the increasing demand for these types of tests. Rather than doing the tests under cover, in a sub-rosa fashion, sensory analysts soon became recognized for providing valuable information. However, they were never really given a budget nor encouraged to interact with professionals outside of their own company. And, in an almost unconscious collusion, the sensory analyst began to perceive himself as a 'supplier' of services to the company, hired and owned by the company, but someone whose value was 'delivering the services cheaply'. In a phrase, sensory analysis became at once the professional who had the answer, the professional without a recognized scientific heritage and, of course, the low cost supplier who believed in his heart of hearts that the real value he offered was low cost testing. The ostensible rationale was science, but the real selling point was low cost.

5. <u>The inevitable consequences – insularity, pigeon-holing, defensiveness, us versus them attitude.</u> The story of sensory analysis brings us to a field that today, in 2009, has become extraordinarily valuable to the corporation. It is the interface between the product developer, quality manager, and the consumer. Company after company created departments filled with sensory analysts. However, since none of us can escape our upbringing, our childhood, and the specifics that may warp our behavior, sensory analysis is no different. Despite the importance of their contributions, these professionals still project that feeling of '*do it yourselfers*', much like the competence of graduate students who have to show that they can do it. These behaviors are manifest in positioning as the low-cost suppliers, and their ability to do all the work alone. In a sense, sensory professionals are still fighting the wars that they fought when the field was developing, even though it has matured.

6. <u>Lessons from sensory analysis for today:</u> The key lesson to be learned about sensory analysis comes from the nature of its discipline in today's corporation. With increasing skills needed for innovation, and the growing movement of open-innovation, companies are recognizing that they can't 'go it alone', that they have to work with outside sources, to play with others. However, sensory analysis has not yet learned that lesson. It continues to maintain an ambiguous position – proclaiming itself at once the expert on product guidance which is necessary for the company, while at the same time serving as the low cost supplier. They can do the work as well as any outside resource, but at a lower price. This ambiguity will eventually hurt the field, and should serve as an object lesson.

<u>Market Research and how it grew</u>
The history of market research both parallels the history of sensory analysis and yet differs from it, with remarkably divergent results. In the 1930's, companies

already recognized that they needed to understand the minds and hearts of consumers. Whether the issue was political, where the knowledge would be used to sway the voter, or product-related where the knowledge would be used to sway customers and please them, astute company managers realized that the customer (or voter) would be king (or queen). This was a change from a subsistence economy, where people would accept essentially anything that was proffered to them, doing so gratefully just to have food on the table.

With this need in mind, and instead of looking at the laboratory where the product developers were creating home-grown methods for measuring food acceptance, let's look at the business part, where marketers and managers were trying to anticipate the customer's needs. The focus was no longer on the product, with the customer being just another 'instrument'. Rather, the focus became the customer, with the product being one part of the mix, as you will see below.

1. A practice, emerging without a systematized body of scientific knowledge: Just as in the case of sensory analysis, there was no systematized body of knowledge about consumers. Companies recognized that they had to understand the consumer, but did not know where to begin. Over time, however, very smart university sociologists began to investigate consumer behavior, and like sensory analysts, published articles in different journals. Of course, readers did not know where to look to find these articles, since the research appeared in scattered, topic-specific journals. Moreover, there were no journals devoted to consumer behavior as such, nor would there be until the American Marketing Association came into being in the 1930's. So here is the first parallel between sensory analysis and market research. Neither emerged out of a rigorous scientific discipline. Both emerged, and hoisted themselves up, by their own bootstraps.

2. Demand that the practitioner be facile in sampling statistics, in a world where statistics savvy was rare, and computational power almost entirely absent: Marketing research meant studying consumers. The statistical basis of that was sociology, political polling and the like. One did not conduct experiments in market research, so there was no experimental design to be considered as part of the knowledge base. The statistics were not focused on discriminating between differences. Rather, the statistics were derived from political polling (what's the margin of error for preferring one product to another). Statistical sampling theory was very important.

3. A collaborative skunkworks. Early market researchers prided themselves on putting together the studies and running them. University professors were called upon to help design the sampling plan and help collect the data. However, there

was less of a sense of 'proving one's competence', perhaps because the marketing researchers were not scientists who were accustomed to doing everything themselves. These researchers worked in teams, as most business people do. Thus, the marketing research culture fostered collaboration. In contrast, the sensory analysis culture, coming from bench science and personal proficiency, fostered the need to prove that 'one could do it oneself'. It is the collaborative mind-set of market research, specifically collaboration within a business environment, which would create the culture of market research as a business tool, rather than as a demonstration of one's personal level of proficiency (i.e., the unwritten code of sensory analysis).

4. The inevitable consequence – market research as a purchasable (i.e., outsourceable) business service: Faced with the need to understand what consumers were doing and, of course, what they wanted, enlightened companies began to hire outside individuals to measure consumers. There was no need to keep this consumer-facing capability in-house. Neither were there real technical secrets, nor, indeed, any home-grown approaches springing forth from the technical staff. Consumer information was perceived to be 'purchasable', meaning it was outsourced to contractors, such as Arthur C. Nielsen, later founder of AC Nielsen, the market research behemoth.

5. The role of market research: Market research became a specialty within marketing. Marketing researchers struggled with the notion of professionalization. They wanted to build credibility in their organizations by solving problems, even when it meant hiring outside talent to do so. Since marketing researchers did not come from the laboratory, from the bench chemists accustomed to doing everything, they had stake in being the least cost supplier. However, that role did not solve business problems, which market researchers focused on rather than gathering more professional acknowledgment for themselves. Certainly, market researchers wanted to acquire a higher status in the industry. They acquired that higher status by contracting with smart people, external suppliers, to get their jobs done, rather than by building staffs that could do everything less expensively. Even companies that once had their own research staffs, such as Procter and Gamble, Unilever, and General Foods, Inc., found it more economical and far better for the business to contract out both the routine work and the high level thinking. There were no threats that such outsourcing would damage their market research image.

6. Lesson from market research for today: The important lesson to keep in mind here is that market researchers 'got it' faster than sensory analysts did. Market researchers realized that they had to 'play well with outsiders', and that it didn't pay to 'compete with suppliers'. The notion that *'anything you can do I can do better'*,

of "*Annie Get Your Gun*" fame, did not apply. For market researchers, it was important for them to keep their eyes on the prize – acceptance by their organizations, leading to promotions, and to jobs well done. And not, as would turn out to be the case, pats on the head for doing the work of six people with a staff of four or five. The goal was to move their businesses ahead by accomplishment, not by saving pennies.

Summing up

The lesson from comparing the two corporate functions, sensory analysis versus market research, is simple. At some time in your career, you are going to face a challenge. The challenge will be whether to be a loner, proving your worth through the corporation, or become a team player, using corporate resources as part of a group. There's no right answer to this question, just lessons to be learned, and issues to be considered. How you begin your career will affect where you go, and how far. You may opt for the science of sensory analysis, or for the business of market research. You may try to combine both, but that third choice, combining two disparate worlds, may turn out to be the equivalent or riding two horses at the same time. You really have to decide who and what you are.

✲ ✲ ✲

PART 4

MAKING YOUR MARK

CHAPTER 16

FIRST ORDER PROBLEMS, SECOND ORDER PROBLEMS, AND THE PAYOUTS

What's important to work on

Newly minted professionals and, in fact, researchers of any sort, don't come fully imbued with wisdom about what's important and what's not important. Reading scientific literature without a critical eye presents you with an array of papers. It's really quite hard to determine which papers are important and which are simply fillers, to be forgotten over time. Even today, there are so many papers, and such a plethora of journals, that even the most experienced professional has trouble knowing what's worth spending time on, and what merely needs to be discarded as irrelevant.

So, how do you know what's important to read? More important, what you should work on? You may not discover the important problems from reading the literature. For one, the scientific literature and, perhaps, all research-based literature in journals, is comprised of stylized papers. There is very little in the way of true individuality in the structure of these papers. Second, the papers all look alike, in terms of having important-sounding titles, with gravitas that may not be deserved or, in the few cases, gravitas that is hidden behind the ritualized authoring and publication processes.

Perhaps the most important thing for a starting researcher to distinguish is an important problem versus a problem that's minor, but whose answer may fill a 'hole in the literature' (whatever that may mean), and which might bring promotion and even tenure when enough are published. The ability to discern first order problems is key for professional success, when you want achievement to be meaningful rather than merely based on a collection of second order, hack-work studies. (By the way, there's nothing wrong with hack-work if that is your proclivity. So, no offense is meant in this chapter to anyone who delights in second-order problems of a gap-filling nature!).

Where do you start?

How does a novice start a research career? If you listen to some relatively 'recent' Ph.D.'s who received their degrees between two and six years ago, and who are now safely ensconced in tenure tracks, or in laboratories somewhere, you may simply want to go home and cry. You may, and the emphasis is may, hear some very disquieting things, such as the fact that these particular individual 'knew' at the outset that the field of endeavor they work in has 'paydirt'.

Well, the truth of the matter is '*it ain't necessarily so*'. No one really knows who will hit paydirt, and what will fizzle, what will excite the scientific mainstream, or what will bore these individuals. Early on in one's career it's often a crap-shoot. Oh, to be sure, there are some areas that are 'hot', but the odds are that any novice in those hot areas is likely to be at the bottom of a very big totem pole, sort of low man or woman, at the base of the feeding chain.

So with these discouraging words, how do you start? What should you do? Is there a magic answer, an optimal strategy, some path that guarantees that you are picking important problems? Or, is it just the luck of the draw, what you end up with, and the winner takes all?

Should you know all the literature?

A lot of researchers begin with searches through the literature, hoping against hope that all of a sudden a big idea will hit. It makes sense, at least at the very beginning, to know the literature of one's field, to understand the kinds of problems that people have faced, and then to sally forth with new efforts.

There's only one problem with knowing the literature. That is, the literature is comprised of efforts that can only rarely be called 'first rate'. Oh, to be sure, in every field there are first rate ideas and major studies. The problem, however, is that science is normative. That is, it tries to hew to a path that is perceived to make a contribution, but not to do something outré. So, there are simply a lot more second rate efforts in normative science than first rate ones. The first rate ones tend to be squashed, simply because they are ahead of their time. And, in normative science, it's often hard to distinguish between 'ahead of its time' and garbage research.

What's the consequence of the dampening effect of normative efforts? What does a profound knowledge of this literature mean for the novice professional? Learning the literature is a job unto itself. It reduces one's anxiety. After all, it is important to know what other researchers have done, so that one's work can fit in the grooves already established.

It's here that the problem starts. To be frank, after the first few major articles, most of the normative research tends to deal with second order problems, done in a rote manner, by professionals following the 'rules'. They are not diverging too far from the accepted norms or accepted wisdom of the particular field. Of course, it didn't start out that way. The stream of scientific literature particular to the problem began with some departure from the norm, spun in a gossamer web in the mind of a non-conformist researcher who managed to get their paper published. Over time, however, the forces of conformity and mediocrity took over. What was a departure from the then current wisdom became in itself the new current wisdom, from which nothing should depart.

So, what is the right thing to do here? Should you first read all of the literature and then dive in? If you do, you're likely to re-shape your ideas, to fit into the literature that comprises a lot of second order, and fairly irrelevant material. If you don't read the literature, more than likely your efforts will be rejected by your colleagues in the scientific community, either for being amateurish or for being arrogant. Amateurs believe, erroneously, that there is nothing out there, and that they are the first to deal with a problem. Arrogant professionals feel the same thing, but they know the literature.

Perhaps the best thing to do is read as much of the literature as you can. However, ask a colleague or, in fact, several colleagues, to recommend what to them would be the best most important papers to read in the field, and especially in the topic areas in which you are working. Asking several colleagues for this recommendation is better than asking one individual alone, because you're likely to get a balanced selection. Furthermore, it's OK to ask colleagues.

When you ask, it would also be a good idea to probe a bit more, beyond just asking for the recommendation, to the 'why' underlying the articles they suggest. Researchers love to discuss other research, other researchers, and other points of view. It's in the DNA of most researchers to evaluate others, to question what others do, and to subtly defend their own efforts while at the same time putting their efforts on par with that of other colleagues or, even, above the efforts of their colleagues. Tap into that.

What is a hypothesis for your research and where does it come from?

By the time you have finished your literature search, you may come up with a number of ideas about what to research. How then do you put these nascent ideas into some type of coherent whole that will guide your research?

Most of us who take degrees in science begin our research with some type of hypothesis. We get these hypotheses by investigating what has been done. When you write for some journals, especially business research journals, you're often asked to state your hypothesis at the start of the paper, and then to show that the research either 'proves' or 'disproves' your hypothesis. We've put the word 'proves' in quotes because the truth of the matter is that one doesn't really 'prove' a hypothesis at all. One collects data that agree with the prediction that one would make from the hypothesis. That's not proof. In many cases, simply luck, and a jaundiced eye which overlooks the evidence that might disprove the hypothesis.

Getting back to our topic, how do you get a hypothesis? Does it emerge fully formed or does it sort of evolve as you work your way through ideas? Is there a universe of hypotheses that can guide you in your research? Clearly there are different ways of getting to a hypothesis, some more 'politically correct' than others. The truth of the matter is that, for the most part, we are not *homo logicus*, logical thinking machines, which work with hypotheses in an orderly, structured manner, declaring first how the world might work, and then studiously applying our intellect to establish or refute the validity of this ingoing idea by deduction from the facts we collect. It's a great story…but, again,' it *ain't necessarily so,'* at least a lot of the time.

The reality of the way we think is quite different. Hypotheses typically come from flashes of insight, from the quiet inside world where all of a sudden you think '*hey..this might be some connection between two variables..if we do A then we might likely get B'*. That's not exactly the inner dialogue, but it's a sufficiently reasonable facsimile.

The notion here, then, is that you'll probably arrive at your working hypothesis in an unexpected way. It won't be in the logical order that you will present it, whether in your thesis or your papers, or even in your discussions with other students. Hypotheses, except for the most boring ones, don't come that way. You may read the journals, but it's in your mind, in the unconscious, where a lot of these factoids combine in a stew. All of a sudden an insight will hit, some inspiration that perhaps this is a 'facet of how the world works'. And, all of a sudden, you've got your hypothesis, after, of course, a bit of reworking so it doesn't sound like the verbatim of a psychotherapy session or the hard-to-follow, but intrinsically well structured, conversation of teenagers.

But how will you recognize it?

It's nice to hear someone talking about hypotheses, science, about being a scientist. And, if you were to have 20+ years, you might find the discussion itself interesting, perhaps in the same way that you enjoy conversations about how hard your childhood was. That relaxed conversation comes when you are no longer anxiety-ridden about being a child, about growing up.

But, the truth of the matter is that most of you who read this chapter will be significantly younger, and more likely to be at the start of their careers, rather than being at the apex or, heaven forbid, on the down-slide later on. So this section is for you. It's not about pontificating, but about how to recognize a hypothesis.

There aren't really any tricks. Perhaps the best advice is to have a conversation with yourself first, talking about the hypothesis you have developed as a series of questions. Does the idea even sound serious? Or is it so complicated that you can't explain it to your mother? This is not a facetious remark. Mothers know a great deal; they love their children. In addition, your mother is sufficiently removed from the inner workings of your research project so that she can give you a fair opinion. Try to make your mother truly and profoundly understand the question you are asking. This understanding should not be the *pro-forma* nodding that comes from colleagues who don't want to look ignorant, or from students who you teach/mentor/grade who don't want to be embarrassed. Nor does it come from siblings who, if the age difference between you two is not particularly great, are probably uncomfortable and downright bored doing this. Your mother never is.

How I spent my summer (developing a Ph. D. hypothesis) – personal recollection (HM)

Since this is a book of presumed wisdom and experience, handed from one genera-tion to another, it's appropriate, when not overdone, to give personal reminiscences. This volume isn't an autobiography by any means. There is room to share with you some of the formative experiences that may be relevant to the topic. And so, this di-gression. From here on, for the rest of the section, the language will be couched in 'I', rather the impersonal 'we', or the even more impersonal 'one'.

It was towards the end of 1966 and the early spring of 1967 that I was cast-ing around for a suitable subject for my doctoral thesis. I was a second year graduate student in the Department of Psychology at Harvard University, virtually living and studying in the impressive 14 story building, William James Hall. Designed by the noted architect, I.M. Pei, the building housed psychol-ogy and social relations departments. It had just opened the year before, in 1965, and I was fortunately or, perhaps, less fortunately, one of the first inhabitants.

In the 1960's we were quite fortunate, at least those of us interested in the 'lower senses' of taste and smell, the field in which I began my career more than forty years ago. Not much was then known about taste, especially about the psychophysics of taste. For sure, there was the clinical literature, as well as the not very available old German literature of a century before. For the most part, little was known with respect to the psychophysics of taste. Much would be discovered later on. However, there I was, a young, 23 year old graduate student, faced with the problem of finding an acceptable topic for a doctoral thesis.

So, how did one go about finding that topic? Harvard did not believe in pro-viding overly-supportive professors to guide the doctoral process. At Harvard Psychology, at least in the 1960's, the sense was that one either swam or sunk. Certainly a professor might, in an off moment of emotional weakness, suggest a topic for a thesis. For the most part, the student was left to fend for himself.

Despite the lack of support, such an indifferent environment can actually help a student. There was no pressure. In fact, there was complete indif-ference, combined with an intellectual integrity that is not often encoun-tered. Professors, especially S.S. (Smitty) Stevens, guided slightly, but weren't *particularly interested in the daily travails of their students, except, of course, for the ultimate integrity of the research. Otherwise, students were expected to do everything themselves.*

I asked myself what I should do. It became clear to me that the best type of problem to work on was one that did not have richness of information attached to it. This choice was a double edged sword. On the one hand, not having any information meant that I would be carving a new path. As a graduate student that could be dangerous. There are no guides, no vade mecae, to inform whether the idea is a good one or a poor one. On the other hand, if there were no experts, no guides, no one who knew, then it was likely that professors didn't know the 'right answer'. The psychophysics of vision and audition were well worked over in 1967. However, the psychophysics of taste (and later of smell) did not have any real experts. So, the decision was obvious. Taste, although relatively empty of psychophysics and more or less lonely at that time, was more attractive to me.

But, let's return to hypotheses! Without guidance, who really knew what was a relevant question, versus what could be just a second order issue about method that had no promise? And so, it was off to the books, to read up on what was then known about taste and smell. And read I did, journal after journal (more in searching than reading, not much published), and book after book (especially R.W. Moncrieff's book, The Chemical Senses, which was the book at the time, despite having been published in the 1940's).

Yet, despite the assiduous efforts, it wasn't clear what a promising hypothesis might be. In fact, the psychophysics of taste and smell were, although not empty, pretty sparse, with only a few papers. There were some individuals working in the field, such as Don McBurney and Linda Bartoshuk. (Linda would eventually become a lifelong friend, but we're getting ahead of the story.)

Reading was critical, but imagination of what could be was even more critical. That wonderful, frightening summer of 1967 saw the inklings of an idea. And, what's more important, since there were no experts around to pooh-pooh it, the idea was able to take root. The notion was that there might be things to learn from taste mixtures. It has to be confessed that this wasn't exactly a novel idea, sprung forth like the goddess Athena from the head of Zeus. Rather, the idea came from reading what was known about taste, from accidental encounters with both the old German literature on it, and with animal literature on taste preferences. Both of those were found in the Harvard Psychology library.

In 1967, little was known about the psychophysics of taste. But, there was some literature. And, as I was studying for the language examination in German that summer, I happened across a reference to an article by the famous German psychophysicist, Emil von Skramlik. Written in the 1920's, the article had the daunting name of "Mischungsgleichungen aus dem Gebiete des Geschmacksinns" (equal intensity mixtures in the field of taste). This was the first half of the key. The second half was a paper by P.T. Young, who had been interested in taste preferences in rats and had done studies on taste mixtures, in the late 1950's. The article was "The pleasantness of mixtures in taste and olfaction".

It's not the articles themselves, but the underlying psychological processes that should be of interest to the reader. How did reading these two articles, among many others, all of a sudden make things 'click'? What was the magic, if any, and what lessons could the reader learn?

Well, the answer isn't a simple one. It's not that all of a sudden, deus ex machina, the hypothesis appeared. It wasn't that the experiments for the Ph.D. materialized from a considered opinion, weighing of alternatives, luxuriating in thought and reverie about scientific contributions to be made. It was nothing of the sort. The actual process was more subtle. It was the clear, yet hard-to-explain, realization that there was pay-dirt in the mixture. It wasn't clear what the pay-dirt was, in fact. It was just intuitively obvious that mixtures were 'rich' in opportunity. The realization was more of a gut feeling, or a feeling in the arm before you're ready to throw a ball. It's a sense of mental rehearsal. Maybe, in fact, it was the relief of tension, like when you knew that there was an answer or when you were lost and then you knew you weren't really lost anymore, although you didn't precisely know where you might be. The exact hypothesis would have to wait.

And so the story continues, not one about a wonderful revelation as an unwriteable story about intuition, feelings. Although there was a sense that mixtures were going to be important, it would be a month or so until the ideas finally crystallized. The study would be similar to other psychophysics studies, only this time with taste mixtures rather than blends of sounds or lights.

What's the moral of this story, of these memories? For one, the moral is that, at least for this author, there was no guidance from top management (i.e., professors) about what was an appropriate problem to work on. There were some discussions, but in the end, it was important to cast around, look at the literature, think of what might suffice for a Ph.D. Second, and perhaps the best thing, was that the research efforts did not fit neatly into a 'hole in the literature waiting to be filled'. The sheer act of reading, of coping with the unknown, of exploring, fantasizing, rather than of specializing in a particular problem, was the real crux of the Ph.D. education. The research was not conducted as part of a general program of someone else's making. And, the hypotheses were not someone else's. Rather, the hypotheses emerged slowly as part of the education of a scientist, rather than a specific 'something to test out' as part of someone else's research program.

And that made all the difference.

On the value of a guidance committee

If the journey to first order problems and, in turn, to one's scientific career is an essentially solo dance with oneself, then what's the value of a committee to guide one's thesis and to help form a hypothesis? This is a very hard question to answer and, perhaps, the answer that may come is not politically correct. Here it is.

In the best of times, one's guidance committee for a Ph.D. serves as a sounding board. In the worst of times, this same committee can create unbearable, occasionally insoluble, problems and insurmountable barriers. When a young scientist is about to write a thesis, the real struggle has to go on inside her/himself. It does little good for a committee and, especially, for a single outstanding, well-funded researcher to take the student under their/his wing, and spoon-feed ideas and encouragement. Certainly, that will work. The committee will assuage their collective egos while the outstanding single researcher gains a new acolyte and, of course, some unpaid labor.

But it's wrong, very wrong. Why? Because that precious time between completing one's coursework and defending the thesis has to be given over to internal growth, to a coming to grips with oneself, to the hero's departure from the land, and the return from the unknown. Committees who hand the student a problem and the advisor who makes the student part of the research team prevent this growth, just as an over-protective parent prevents the child from developing the inner self confidence that the child needs to go on with life.

And just what happens to the student who is protected, given the problem by the committee and who works dutifully and faithfully as a member of a research team? Well, for one, the student may never undergo the inside struggle which is so vital to creating the scientist. We may have a well trained person, but one who is missing something, perhaps courage, vision or confidence. The student may receive a Ph. D., but go on to a life of second order problems, afraid of or, perhaps, better without the necessary tools to deal with new ideas, new visions, new ways of doing things.

It's all inside. You won't know whether you are a member of a team (and what that implies), or a lone ranger, an individual, a person, ready to take on the challenge of scientific problems. That is, you won't know until you're faced with a problem. Then what do you do? Will you long for the team for the support or for the camaraderie? Or, will you pick yourself up, and plan the hows and ways you will need to meet this new challenge? You'll know it when it hits you; it always does, sometime in your life.

✵ ✵ ✵

CHAPTER 17

LEARNING TO THINK AND TO FEEL

Introduction – facing different scientific mind-sets

Diversity is the rule of nature; it also holds sway in the realm of science. What a terribly boring world this would be if all scientists were to think the same thing, in the same way. But they don't. That's why there are reviewers for journals, critics for art works (no doubt masterpieces), and different flavors of tea and pasta sauces. '*Of taste one does not dispute*'.

But, what about the student? How does the student, and then the young profes-sional, cope with the plethora of opinions? Who of us with a decade or more of ex-perience in the field has not had the joy of an almost knock-down, drag-out fight with a colleague, perhaps verbal, but with that desire to shake some sense into the other person, our antagonist? Can't he or she see the correctness of our opinion?

There are different mind-sets in science. We're not just talking about beliefs in how the world works, but about different ways that scientists approach their task. On the one hand, we have the hypothetico-deductive type, strictly rational, looking for simple, easy to demonstrate, cause and effects. Change one variable, and another measure changes. Do the experiment a sufficient number of times (boredom nothwithstanding), demonstrate that the effect is robust, and suddenly you have a paper. In fact you have more than a paper. You have a very satisfied investigator, who has demonstrated a fact of reality or, perhaps more than one wishes to admit, a factoid of reality. The literature is filled with these factoids. Read enough and you get to see how the world works in your specific area. It isn't necessarily inspiring, but it is absolutely rock solid. You could rest your career comfortably on these facts, established meticulously, documented, re-ported, and quantified to within an inch of their lives. This is normative science. There's a lot of it to be read.

And yet, there is the other type, the one whose story reads a bit like a fairy tale or, perhaps, like the inspiration one might get from a heroic narrative poem (i.e., Tennyson's *Mort d'Arthur*). This poetic approach to science involves the researcher making leaps from problem to problem, with sparks, insights, dashing here and there. We're not talking about the phonies, the '*zeitgeister shyster*' (to quote a term from the 1960's). We're not talking about the showman full of persiflage, but rather about the true visionary who discerns the pattern underneath the data and who dares wrestle with nature, coming out ahead.

Both approaches to science are valid. Of course, nature doesn't distribute these approaches equally. There are a lot more of the first type, the normative scientists, the ones who produce well documented papers that are statistically sound and, in doing so, lay down the knowledge base of the science. There are a lot fewer of the second type; often those are misunderstood. They are not the 'neat and tidy types', the 'buttoned down' researchers who are careful to cross their t's and dot their i's. They are a different type, more poets than plodders, more visionaries than practitioners.

Science needs both types. Neither is better than the other; they're simply different.

Tough minded versus tender minded science

You have no doubt heard of tough minded versus tender minded in science, business, and in life. William James, one of the doyens of psychology in the late 19th century, characterized researchers as belonging to one of these two groups. The differentiation has stuck. Even today, more than a century later, look at Google® for citations about 'tough minded versus tender minded' and you'll find about 140 of these listed. And, in Google Scholar®, you'll find about 50 of these citations.

Tough and tender produce two distinct images in one's mind. Tough 'feels' critical, hard, rigid, highly judgmental, with a sense of right. Tender feels open, warm, and, perhaps, not particularly disciplined, accepting, but certainly not nasty.

So which is it going to be? There is something to be said for both mind-sets in science. Of course, many people want to feel tough minded. It seems so strong, so righteous. Tough minded is what science is all about, isn't it? Doesn't science pride itself in a self-correcting mechanism, by which the incorrect ideas are weeded out, leaving only that which is demonstrably repeatable and correct?

And then, there is tender-minded. Tender-mindedness gives us a sense of lack of criticism, of a *touchie-feelie* that might be appropriate for clinical psychologists, but is certainly not the appropriate stance to take when one is uncovering the 'secrets' of the world.

What's in it for you

When you read reviews of papers, especially those you write, you will be struck by the degree of tough-mindedness that seems to come over reviewers when they are asked to comment on another's work and judge the fitness of it for the archival scientific literature. It seems as if the reviewer adopts an even tougher attitude, a carapace of the mind, in their attempt to protect the innocence and reputation of science. We have all been subject to such reviews at one or another time. Of course, many of us will no doubt live to enjoy a greater number in the future.

Although there is a proclivity in young scientists to be tough minded (and the writer was certainly one of them), being tender minded isn't a bad thing, if one behaves judiciously. Tender-mindedness in a young scientist means s/he is sensitive to others, going beyond the minutiae of one's science and perceiving the 'soul' inside oneself and, at the same time, inside the other. It's a matter of being kind, understanding, compassionate to oneself first as budding young professional, but then to others, who are struggling with the same problems of becoming who they are meant to be.

And just how, you ask, does one become a bit more tender-minded in a world which seemingly values toughness, rigorousness, exactitude, and a punishing attitude toward failure? The trick is not to accept second rate work, to occasionally let mistakes pass, to be kind and 'leave no researcher behind', no 'paper unpublished'. Perhaps, the best way to become tender minded in a world of toughness is to give the other person, the other researcher, the proverbial 'benefit of the doubt'. As in Ethics of the Fathers, a perennial favorite among Jews for righteous living, '*be in the state of mind to judge others and their work on the scale of merit*.' By the way, this doesn't mean accepting garbage, but rather being fair, as you might have the other be fair to you.

The truth of the matter is that your own scientific work will not be compromised, nor your great (or, more truthfully, irrelevant) reputation tarnished when you act gently towards others. When you review, look to guide, not to express your superiority because it's a blind review. Be ready to help, to add, to encourage others. You'll do better science if you seek to improve rather than search to destroy.

✡ ✡ ✡

CHAPTER 18

COLLABORATING IN RESEARCH AND IN WRITING

Introduction

It's in the nature of many, indeed most people, to collaborate on research and then to publish papers together. And, in many cases, collaborating is fun. Finally, in a world where the number of publications is important for obtaining tenure or grants and where bean counting is well respected in science (include sophisticated methods such as impact scores), collaborating is a quick way to raise one's production.

That being said, how do you go about collaborating with someone? In the world of science and, of course, in the world of publishing, everyone has an *amour propre*, an image of oneself. How do you get to work with people, when you realize that each person is effectively competing with every other person, if not for resources, then for recognition and fame?

Perhaps, the best way to begin any collaboration is to become friends with the other individual. It doesn't hurt to have lunch together, to chat at coffee, to have breakfasts and so forth. It's also important that during these set-up meetings, prior to the collaboration, each person clearly recognizes that there is value in collaborating, so that one person doesn't feel hard done by or taken advantage of. These often unspoken, but negative feelings can kill a long term relationship and neuter the meaningfulness of the collaboration. You should accentuate the positive and see how both or all parties can benefit. But that, of course, is common sense. You have to repeat it to yourself, but in truth there's nothing new here except the obvious.

Let's move to the less obvious

It Is ok, even admirable, to want to collaborate. But, why do some collaborations go on for years, while others last the length of one or two papers, and others die a horrid death, even before a paper or data are produced? What's the secret sauce in collaboration? Or is there one? Is the sauce in the chef, the researcher, or is the sauce in the topic, what is being investigated?

These are hard questions; there's no answer. However, look around. Look at your colleagues who have been in the field for 10, 20, 30 or even 40 years. How do they operate? With whom do they collaborate? What are they doing, and why? Have you ever thought of asking them why they collaborate or don't collaborate? Or, what goes right, what goes wrong?

We begin with the people. For successful collaboration to go on for more than the momentary itch, momentary passion and intellectual infatuation, each person has to know his (and, of course, her) position in the collaboration. Not all collaborations are equal, of course. So, it's not a matter of each person being the leader half the time, or some other such formula that you might think is the secret to success. Collaboration is like a marriage or a dance. Each party should know its role, and just as importantly, recognize that the role is what it is. It's no use for two married people to compete about who is boss, or who does what. They can discuss, but not compete. The marriage breaks down. Nor can two people who dance together both lead at the same time. They may feel equal, but they can't dance together.

Now that we know a bit about collaboration, let's delve into it more deeply, examining the motives for working together. Why specifically do YOU want to collaborate? This isn't necessarily an easy answer, nor is it one single answer. Is it because you feel uncertain of yourself? Feelings of fear, uncertainty, especially when one begins a career, are not all that unusual. In fact, the person who looks calm at the start of the career, who seems to 'know' the right moves and what to do may, in fact, be totally wrong, and may miss the boat entirely. No person is an island, and no one really '*knows it all*', not even when the person is at the pinnacle or even later, at end of the career, rather than at the beginning. So, it's perfectly OK to collaborate because you are unsure of yourself. In fact, it is probably a better idea to collaborate than to hide your possible ignorance by withdrawing into yourself.

There may be something else, some Machiavellian reason for collaborating. That's OK as well. We don't necessarily collaborate out of fear or diffidence. We may collaborate in order to gather together a string of publications. With achievement in scientific research counted in terms of quantity as well as quality, collaborating with others is a quick way to build up one's resume. Certainly at this point, you are probably recoiling at the sheer thought of 'using others', of 'padding a resume'. Well, get over it. The reality is that you are living in a world filled with carnivores, herbivores, and omnivores. It's a world of eat or be eaten, publish or suffer the consequences. There's absolutely nothing wrong with a bit of publishing behavior where you attach yourself to the coattails of others. That is, nothing wrong if this happens at the start of your career, where the harshest taskmaster on you may be yourself. It's quite wrong, however, if this attachment to the research team and collaboration characterizes most of your career, instead of just its beginning.

And then there is the collaboration of equals, of true team spirit, of kindred souls who work together, share ideas and share authorship. That's probably the best collaboration. It's the story of the selfless friendship between Damon and Pythias of Greek mythology, or of Jonathan and David of the *Old Testament*. Here's the best of the world, where each of the collaborators can do more together than they could alone. Here is where science may reach new heights. And, indeed, in the *Ethics of the Fathers*, it is written '*make for yourself a judge; buy yourself a friend*'. The price of purchase could well be collaboration; not a bad price either.

Who is likely to collaborate?

When we look at the scientific literature, searching for collaborating partners, what types of patterns do we see? You ought to try the experiment, looking for papers that are authored by one, two, three, and then four or more individuals. Then, ask yourself what types of patterns you observe, and what do they mean? What do you sense is going on here? Don't look at today's researchers; you're too involved emotionally, you may not like some of the protagonists, and your judgment will be a bit clouded and biased. Instead, look at the research from 20 and 30 years ago to get a sense. Obviously, there are many different areas of science where people might publish, as well as different topic areas open for collaboration. Yet, when you stand back, you might see something like this:

1. <u>One-author papers with a strong bent of theory.</u> These are often major papers of a theoretical sort although, of course, not always. A lot of very important theory papers seem to be written by one author, even when, as a general rule, the author tends to collaborate with others. If this observation is true, then why do you think it happens? A good possibility is that people do not like to collaborate when they set forth ideas that they believe to be critical, even 'game changing'. Despite the professionals' affiliation need, which leads to collaboration, all are not selfless. When an experienced researcher feels that he is 'on to something big', you won't see collaboration. You're more likely to see a relatively longer, one-author paper, even if that single authorship is out of character.

2. <u>Papers that seem to be the 'next' or nth iteration of a particular topic.</u> These papers seem to be laying the groundwork for the field by yet another parametric study. These studies, the bedrock of normative science, do not break new ground as much as fill in the gaps of knowledge. They extend what we know in a quantitative or qualitative manner. These papers tend to be, more often than not, shared by several researchers. Again, the reason will become clear when we think about the contributions of these papers. The papers don't break ground. Rather, they are the basis of normative science. No one establishes a career or reputation by authoring these papers, other than by being appreciated as a competent researcher.

3. <u>Papers that deal with equipment or methodological issues.</u> These papers almost always have several authors. They present the use of new pieces of equipment or methods for analyzing data. There are some good reasons why these methods papers have several authors. One reason is that they are usually very

simplistic papers. They present facts and approaches, but not as new ideas. They are simpler because they are sharing a method or a piece of equipment, rather than trying to understand the world. There is usually not much glory in such papers. A second reason is that such methods usually result from the collaboration of different individuals, so the paper is a good way to reward the collaborators. A final reason is that the papers typically appear in methods journals, which do not generate a lot of professional prestige, unless the method becomes 'hot' and leads to major discoveries. At that point, you're likely to see individual authorships using the method, but published quickly on 'hot new topics'.

So what should YOU do?

Given the nature of professional collaboration, it is probably a very good idea to have a number of early papers where you are a co-author. No one will expect you to have great ideas early in your career. And, when you collaborate, it's a way of showing the scientific community that you are a team player, that you understand the rules, and that you are ready to 'play well with others'.

Over time, however, you will be better off becoming the first author, where you publish a number of papers which are yours alone, and when you begin to separate the topics you write about alone from the topics that you wrote about as part of the team. These steps establish your own identity, separate from the collaborative team of which you are a part. To the degree that you can do both, collaborate with others on some topics, but be the first/solo author on papers dealing with other topics. This will help you establish your own identity. The collaboration will show you as a member of the community, while the solo papers will demonstrate that you have come of age intellectually and professionally.

Just what do you do when you collaborate?

Now that we know why people collaborate, the next question is 'what is collaboration?' It's always a good idea to start something like this question with a quote from somewhere. It makes the writing all the easier, by creating a 'straw man', which one can comment on, expand upon, or take issue with. So, let's begin with Wikipedia's® definition of collaboration:

> *Collaboration is a recursive process where two or more people or organizations work together intersection of common goals — for example, an intellectual endeavor that is creative in nature — by sharing knowledge, learning and building consensus. Collaboration does not require* <u>leadership</u> *and can sometimes bring better results through* <u>decentralization</u> *and* <u>egalitarianism</u>*. In particular, teams that work collaboratively can obtain greater resources, recognition and reward when facing competition for finite resources. . . .*

Structured methods of collaboration encourage <u>introspection</u> of behavior and communication. These methods specifically aim to increase the success of <u>teams</u> as they engage in collaborative <u>problem solving</u>. Forms, rubrics, charts and graphs are useful in these situations to <u>objectively</u> document <u>personal traits</u> with the goal of improving performance in current and future projects.

The basic thought that we derive from the preceding Wikipedia® article is that collaboration occurs between free-standing individuals who are assumed to be somewhat independent. Collaboration can occur between individuals in the same organization. The key is that collaboration occurs between independent individuals, although the nature of the independence is not clearly spelled out. Both individuals can work for the same company, but it is clear that each individual brings something 'unique' to the relationship. There is also a sense of a temporariness of the relationship on which they are collaborating. But the key word is not even spelled out. The key word is *<u>separateness</u>*. Separate individuals collaborate. Or, if they collaborate, they are in a sense separate.

The tonality of the Wikipedia® definition teaches an important life lesson for the young researcher. When you collaborate, you are not your colleague's research assistant. A research assistant and a professional do not really collaborate, unless, for that moment, they are considered separate and, in some respects, equal to each other, even if only for a very short, temporary period of time.

And so you, as a young professional, are momentarily equal when you collaborate, even with an older, far more established professional colleague. Strange as it may seem, in that moment of collaboration ,you are equal co-investigators. Your opinion is valuable and you may well influence the course of the research and the course of writing the paper.

You will experience immense personal growth when you collaborate. By personal growth, we are not referring to establishing greater professional credentials and achievements. Rather, we are talking here of an inner growth, of professional maturation, where you have a chance to stretch yourself, to discover and then nurture the resources inside you that have matured as you became a professional. You bring these to the collaboration as a *rite de passage*. The colleague with whom you collaborate may not even realize it because much of the growth from the collaboration is private, in your soul. Your senior colleague is there for the ride and serving as a mentor, perhaps without being conscious of the transformation going on inside you.

<u>Doing experiments versus writing up experiments</u>

Now that you've decided to collaborate and have done the experiments, your next task is to write up the data in a form appropriate either for a technical report, or better, for a journal. Indeed, the major reason for you to collaborate with people not in your business or academic employer is to add to your resume. There are, of course, situations where the collaboration is fun, especially between colleagues who have known each other for many years and like working with each other. But, for the most part, collaboration has its utilitarian dimension. It is this utilitarian dimension that we explore now, as we deal with writing.

You might think that writing research papers is fairly straightforward. After all, just look at the thousands, tens, and even hundreds of thousands of papers written by collaborating scientists. It doesn't take a genius to realize that people can collaborate. So, what's the trick here? What should you expect? And what are the pitfalls?

Although people collaborate in research, writing up research differs a great deal from doing it. When you do research, you set up the test stimuli and measuring instruments, you make the measurements, and then you record the data. There is not very much that you can do, other than follow the appropriate protocol. Of course, there might be some differences in what each of you believes the appropriate protocol to be but, by and large, those differences can be easily ironed out. Furthermore, it's possible to diverge on executing the experiment, but such divergences are more an example of poor research abilities (more cruelly, poor experimenter abilities) than they are of divergent opinions. Running an experiment is typically done one way, the right way.

When it comes time to write up the results, the different world-views of the collaborators come into sharp relief. This is true, unless, of course, you have been collaborating for a long time, in which case your differences have been ironed out and some *modus vivendi* arrived at. It's sort of like a long-term marriage which works because both partners know what to do, what's expected, and where the boundaries are.

The real problems in collaboration come from when the world views of the different collaborators clash with each other. What is the paper about? That sounds like a fairly simple, straightforward question. The truth is, however, that it's a minefield waiting to blow up the unwary trespasser. To one of the members of the team, the paper is, perhaps, the evidence that the problem is worth working on. Therefore, that individual cites lots of papers to show where, specifically, the problem fits into the general stream of science. To another member, the problem one works on might be worth only a scientific note, rather than a full-fledged paper. And so the debate goes on; what is the appropriate depth for the paper (full treatment of a major problem vs minor topic), what are the conclusions (general implications vs simple specific factoids), how deep should the statistical treatment extend (excruciatingly detailed vs cursory to show the major point, and that's all).

When all is said and done, collaborating is easiest when there are things to DO, and hardest when there are things to WRITE. Writing, in a way, triggers insecurities and tends to bring out people's motivations and create tensions. Whereas doing things is mechanical, motoric, instinctive, the act of writing things is intellectual, fear-generating, and a learned skill.

Okie dokie -- Who gets to write what?

Now that we have drawn a line in the sand, and talked about writing as the point where the collaboration may reach a rocky stage, the next issue to deal with is who gets to write what. There are different collaboration styles. In some of the more successful styles, one person writes the method, the other writes the literature search and some of the discussion.

At the beginning of your collaboration, you may find it VERY productive to discuss who will do what. It sounds a bit pedantic and controlling, but it is certainly not that at all. When two or more people are to create something, they cannot do it completely separately, and then hope to merge the two works into a single coherent document. Having gone through many such attempts over the years, it is clear that the better way is to decide, ahead of time, specifically who among you will be the lead author, and follow a specific sequence of activities.

It's important to establish a sequence in which to write the paper. Two competing tendencies emerge when writing. Both have to be reckoned with:

1. Amicable division of labor based on expertise, perhaps leading to an unfocused paper with too many 'voices': The first tendency of authors is to do one little section of the paper. This first tendency, compartmentalizing, comes from fear or, perhaps, a little from laziness. We tend to do that which makes us feel most comfortable. It's easiest for those who know the literature to write the literature review section and, perhaps, that part of the discussion which pertains to the way the study fits the current literature. It's easiest for the statistician to write the statistical analysis of the data, sometimes following the lead of the individual who fits the study into the stream of other research, but all too often, going off into the world of statistics where it's more comfortable for that statistician. It's a lot easier to emit streams of statistical treatments, which are really tabulated results organized into the hard and boring prose of a scientific paper.

2. Artistic purity, a single focus, perhaps leading to conflict: The second tendency, just as frequent, is to want to write the paper in one's own way, with one's own world view. If two professionals of equal stature write the same paper, in parallel, using the same data but permitted the statistics that they think to be 'appropriate', it's quite likely they'll deal with entirely different papers which

cannot be easily merged. Then, the task is not merely a matter of inter-weaving paragraphs from one and the other. The end result will be unreadable.

Perhaps the best approach is to have one person responsible for the first draft of the paper. It is advisable that the author of the first draft (not necessarily the first in the author sequence) be the better of the writers. A good professional first draft makes all the remaining work move more quickly. The first draft author puts the structure of the paper into place, allowing the other author(s) to edit and add to the skeleton. The paper comes together more quickly, following the basic outline or lineaments set down by the first draft author. All in all, it's not a bad strategy to follow when the final goal is to get the paper out and published in the public domain.

<u>Telling your co-author unpleasant truths – he/she isn't right</u>

By the term 'unpleasant truth' we don't mean anything personal about your co-author, but rather the word 'NO'. Over many years, professionals in the 'business' have all sorts of collaborators. They bring to the collaboration talent , but also maddening things, which the French lovingingly call an *idee fixe* and which, in Yiddish, has the wonderful, zesty name *meshugas* (individual craziness). By this we mean a belief that the world HAS to work in a certain way, the paper HAS to be written in a certain format, the analysis HAS to incorporate certain types of statistics, and so forth. You get the idea.

Disabusing research collaborators of their long-held and fondly-held beliefs is not exactly the easiest thing to do. Perhaps one of the reasons for the difficulty lies in their lack of deep and long-term experience in research and scientific writing. As such, many individuals fall back on a belief that things must happen in a certain way, and that it is the requirement to follow that 'certain way' without deviating. Examples include the absolute necessity of performing statistical 'tests' (it's not science without some probability value from a 't' test or an analysis of variance). Or, it's not science if the paper is written in a chatty, relatively easy to read, almost informal manner, since the paper lacks the gravitas of science. Or, when the paper has too few respondents then, of course, the results cannot be assumed to 'hold water' or be scientificly valid. And, finally, the paper has to be written in a certain style, with all the methods in one section, all the findings (results) in the next section, all the discussions in a third section, even if at the end of the paper the reader is so overwhelmed with minute detail as to forget the thrust of the paper and, in due course, a moment or two, abandons the paper for some other more interesting activity. Rigidity of belief is wonderful in the absence of the moderating wind of experience.

With these 'issues' in mind, how do you disabuse your collaborator, so that you can proceed with a paper that's readable, meaningful to you both (or all), that might even be elegant? One way *not* to proceed is to compromise on every single point, so that the paper looks like the product of a committee. As in any artistic endeavor, for that is what writing is about, you ought to have one voice, one style, one vision. If you're lucky, the style will be clear, the vision sufficiently crisp to attract the reader and the voice sufficiently unitary. If you're not so lucky, you'll have a paper like many other papers. It will be filled with the observations of the many, whose abstract is read, but the body of which defies all but the most assiduous graduate student. That's not a happy state of affairs albeit, and unfortunately, a very common one.

Should you be the first author? What are the rules?

Like everything else where egos get in the way, writing a paper together (or a book) brings up the question of 'who goes first'. The reason is quite simple. Most people remember the first author. So, when you want to establish your reputation, you make almost every effort to have your name first on a number of papers. Of course, when you're not really interested in fame and fortune, or if you've written a lot of papers before and established your reputation, then being first author isn't so important.

There are some unwritten rules. Here are four:

1. When you do a clear majority of the work, you ought to be the first author.

2. When you are simply a collaborator such as a statistician doing service work for the project, you ought not to be the first author, and generally are not, unless the paper deals with new statistical approaches to the topic that YOU have pioneered or at least led.

3. When several people feel that each has contributed equally, all bets are off, and it is a matter of negotiation.

4. When you want to collaborate again with these individuals, or want to establish yourself as a person with whom collaboration is enjoyable, you should figure out a *modus vivendi*, a strategy for several papers, where at least once your name will be first, but on the others your name will be second, or even third or fourth.

You should always keep in mind that despite the apparent adulthood of all the collaborators with whom you work, you are treading into areas laden with landmines. You can, with the wrong move, bring out the insolent child, the needy-for-praise adolescent, the crazy plotting schemer and, of course, the inept bumbler. By insisting that you be first, you may produce feelings of hostility in others. Insisting that another person be first might also produce a great deal of anxiety. Grabbing the first position by the inability of others to 'in-fight' could well lead to a lifetime of bad feelings.

So, at the end of the day, be sensitive to others. Are you in this field for a few years or a lifetime? If so, manage the order of authorship and, indeed, the nature of the collaboration as if your professional career depends upon it. It does. Graciousness and kindness here may pay substantial dividends in the years to come. You don't have to be first to come out ahead.

Who do you cite, and why citing yourself too much angers everyone except your mother

If the order of authors' names isn't problem enough, a second and more pernicious problem is the citations in the reference section. It is here, in the references, all too often unread, that you move beyond insulting each other and perhaps slight other professionals in the field. Let's face it; each of us who writes papers feels that our work is important, at least those of us who make a habit of writing a fair amount. And, we all want to be recognized for what we do. Recognition often comes in the form of citations. It is a matter of who is citing our papers. Secondarily , it is the light or tone in which the specific paper is presented to the reader. There are citation indices that show the impact of each person's contribution. These citation schemes are used to quantify a person's importance. They seem to have some face validity. If you think this is minor, go beyond science and publishing. You can browse the internet and locate Google's 'Alert' service which tells you whenever something specific about you has appeared on a website.

So, let's return to the topic of literature citations in papers. When writing a paper you ought to place it in the context of other scientific work of the same type. Even, of course, if you believe that your efforts sprang up fully formed, like Athena who sprang fully formed from the head of Zeus. Of course, that's never the truth. All scientific research builds on the effort of others. We don't live in a vacuum.

When you cite others, you place yourself into a stream of research. We're not talking about the 'truth' of your contributions, nor about the real location of your efforts in the stream of science. The future will take care of that, if your paper manages to reach the public. Rather, we're talking about how you manage to put your paper into this stream, the specifics, the conscious thoughts about how you want it to be perceived in the history of your field if you don't get totally forgotten first. It is these considerations that will dictate what you cite, who you cite, and how you cite.

1. <u>Citing everyone</u>: The hallmark of a novice scientist, eager to please, is to cite everyone who might possibly read the paper as a reviewer. This obsessive behavior is easy to understand. Graduate students are typically held in subservient positions in their universities. The graduate student must please the professor. One way to do this is by 'aping' the professor, through citing the professor's work. A graduate student soon learns that one way to curry favor is to make a

big to do about 'understanding' the importance of the work of one's professor, generally one who sits on one's committee. This obsequious behavior carries over to the obsessive citation of one's professor, and other potentially 'powerful' senior professionals, in one's early publications.

2. <u>Citing oneself</u>: At the other end of the spectrum is the belief that one's own work deserves citation. To some extent, citing oneself reduces anxiety that is in the background of a researcher's mind. There is the perennial fear of disappearing, of becoming nothing. Citing oneself in the reference section reduces that fear of disappearing. It is the scream of saying '*I'm here, I'm here, look at what I've done*'. Beyond that, there exists a caricature of behavior, wherein one cites one's papers in a seemingly *ad infinitum* way. To tell the truth, there are positives and negatives. On the negative side, there is the irritation. On the positive side, is the often correct point of view that one's own work defines this particular, minute area of research. And, why bother citing others, when the reality in your mind is that their work is second rate? You have to decide what to do. The best thing to do is to cite no fewer than two of your papers and no more than three. That number doesn't irritate, especially if your citations have you as the second or third author, not just the first author. This author's advice – step gingerly, look around, use common sense, and realize that the world is not about you, despite what your mother said when she told you how proud she was of you.

3. <u>Citing older papers or just recent papers</u>? If you have followed the different points in this chapter you may have noticed that there is no clear resolution about what to cite, who to cite, should you cite yourself, and so forth. Another recurring issue is what specifically you should cite. Should you provide a historical retrospective on the problem, or merely refer the reader to previous papers, and cite current work? It's not an easy question to answer. Some journal editors prefer to work only with the latest, up-to-date citations, in an effort to show that the articles in the journal are *au courant*, keeping pace with the times. Other journal editors prefer a more scholarly approach, one that is sufficiently succinct so that you end up citing relevant historically important references. Still other editors don't really care. Again, citations are a matter of opinion. It's a complex dance among three groups – the authors, the journal editors (who represent policy), and the reviewers.

<u>Summing up</u>

Collaborating can be fun. It can be some of the most fun you'll have in your career. What better way to share a future than with colleagues? And, you get to do only half the work, not all of it.

But, before you collaborate, search inside yourself. Know why you are collaborating. Determine what YOU bring to the party. In the end, you will be creating your own career. Collaboration, like marriage, can bring out the best in you. Or, if things go awry, it can bring out parts of you that you would prefer remain concealed.

In any event, know thyself. Then, move forward. And have fun.

✵ ✵ ✵

CHAPTER 19

MECHANICS – WRITING AND PRESENTING
TO BE READ AND UNDERSTOOD

Introduction

Some people like data, while others don't like data. Some people like lots of words and others prefer clean, crisp lines, with a few words put together in exquisitely spare lines. There's no one correct style for presenting data. Each of the foregoing styles has merit, whether graphs, tables, words galore or laconic description.

So, when it comes to presenting your results in a crisp, coherent way, how should you do it? We're not talking about text, but about graphs and tables. You have your data. Now what?

Let's dig a bit deeper. There are clearly people who think in pictures, while there are others who prefer tables, and still others who prefer long expositions of what happened. Which should you use, and why?

Discovering styles of presenting data

Perhaps the best way to discover styles in presenting data is to read a dozen papers in different journals. Of course, the papers will deal with different topics but, for the most part, the authors in a single journal will have more in common with each other than you might expect because they are all writing for a common themed journal. Styles vary by journal, even among commonly themed ones.

As you read the articles, look at the presentation of results. While some of the topics may be the same, each individual author, or more correctly each paper, has its own unique style. You might begin this part of your scientific and research education by visiting a library, preferably a research library, when you can examine a dozen 'numbers' of this single topic journal.

Once you have viewed the different styles of writing and presenting data, you can go back and create your own. Which style feels most comfortable when YOU write? Do you enjoy a few quickly drawn graphs which you believe get to the heart of the point? If so, then point out the specific graphs in the paper, and do a diagnosis. What's special about THESE particular graphs that make you feel that you should use graphs like them? Is it the fancy graphics tools which you believe add pizzazz and sizzle to the paper? Or is it the elegance of the graph? Do you see more in the graph than initially meets the eye, so that the graph continues to deliver? If you can, point out specifically, or even better, write your point of view.

To get a sense of what graphs communicate, or fail to communicate, look at the four graphs in Figure 19.1. The graphs happen to be taken from the advertising for StatPoint Technologies, Inc., a company specializing in computer graphing programs for statistical data, like StatGraphics (www.statgraphics.com).

Four graphs created using StatGraphics computer graphing software

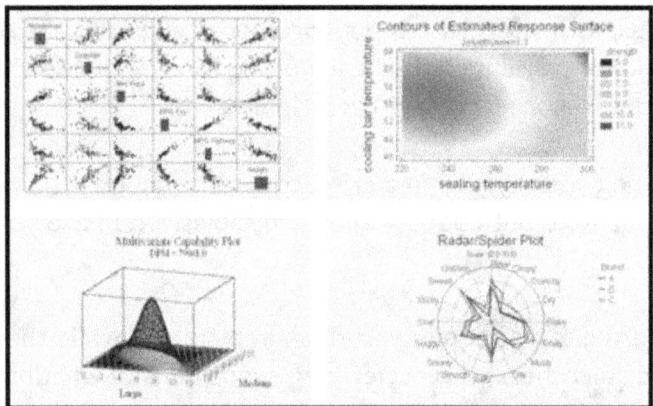

Figure 19.1: Four graphs, computer-plotted, showing how commercially available programs can turn tables of data into pleasing and often insight figures. The plots come from the advertising from StatGraphics (www.Statgraphics.com).

With the easily accessible power of graphing now available in virtually all statistical packages, the real question is not what or how to graph, but why to graph instead of presenting numerical data? You might ask yourself a simple question, "What does this graph tell me or, really, the reader, that I cannot easily get from the text?" Or "what new insights come from this graph?"

You'll notice that the emphasis here is not on formally creating the graph to display results, but rather YOU as the author being conscious of the graph, of what it says, of the effect that it has on the viewer, and its ability to summarize facts. You'll also develop the critical faculty to see that sometimes the graphs are just 'not right'. The data are there, but the graph lacks the impact that you'd like them to have.

A few last cautions about graphs before we move on to presenting data in tables. When you begin to play with graphs, you'll undoubtedly be entranced by the dozens of different graphs that you can easily create. Just look at statistical packages such as SYSTAT®, a favorite of the author's. You need only go to the graphics portion of the package, and follow the drop down menus, to reach a rich assortment of different ways to present your data.

If you're like most people, you will begin to play a bit with some of the graphs. The truth of the matter is, playing is just fine. You need to explore these graphs. You probably won't realize the power, or the clutter, unless you play. You'll eventually find a small group of graphs which best fit the type of data that you will present. And, at the end of it all, you'll most likely settle on 2-4 different graph styles, which you will use for years to come. The experimentation will then evolve to using colors, fills, types of labels, font sizes, and so forth. Like most of us, you'll probably soon tire of feature-richness.

It wasn't always so easy – a short historical digression

> *As a historical aside, this abundance of capability wasn't always the case. We didn't always have automatic graphing of data that could be done and erased in a moment, simply to see 'what the data look like'. Before the great popularity of personal computers, starting in the late 1970's, people had to create their own graphs using templates, India ink, and a light box which projected a light through a translucent plastic cover. The entire system was set up so that the user would first create the graph using pencil on conventional graph paper. Satisfied with the results, the user would then put tracing paper over the graph. The light box made it possible to see the graph, and to trace it using India ink with the appropriate pen (Kohlnoor). The end result was a manual work of art that could take a hour or two. For the fearful, India ink, which was indelible, could be replaced by press-on lettering. Applying that lettering was an equally tedious chore. However, there was no worry of spilling ink. There was just the worry of running out of certain letters and having to buy another set of lettering.*

> *This was quite a different experience from today's rapid-fire creation of graphs!*

> *Yet, in retrospect, the manual efforts may have educated more than today's automated efforts. The reason is simple. The manual system placed effort on thinking, on the inner game, on knowing what should work, because the actual production of the graph was an effort. No one wanted to waste that effort, so one thought a great deal, and only then proceeded to create a graph. Unfortunately, those days are long gone, not to return.*

Presenting data – tables have their place, and it's an honored one

If graphs are so 'neat and cool', so gripping and glitzy, and present so much information, then what's the role of tables of data? Although this seems to be a merely theoretical issue of taste, it's actually much more important. Understanding the nature of data and how to best present detailed results teaches you a great deal about communicating.

When are data tables called for in a paper? Most studies report the results of experiments which test hypotheses. The researcher sets up the conditions of the experiment, 'runs' the appropriate number of subjects through the test conditions following the research protocol, makes the measurements, and then applies statistics.

If the stimuli are just a few unrelated conditions, it's hard to graph these conditions. However, one could create a histogram, showing how these limited set of stimuli perform. For example, think of four beverages as variations of the ever popular 7-Up®, perhaps varying in levels of sweetener and carbonation. The respondents or subjects (the words are interchangeable) rate liking. At the end of the experiment, the researcher measures the response of 100 individuals to the four beverages, and has four numbers, each number being the average liking assigned by those 100 respondents to one of the four beverages. This is the standard type of research.

How should the researcher present these data? Does it really make sense to create a figure with a histogram, showing the four beverages, with the height of the beverage representing the degree of liking? Look at Figure 19.2. What do you learn? Do you understand the data better with the figure (Figure19. 2) than you do with the table (see Table 19.1)?

Data from four beverages

Table 19.1: Presenting the data from four beverages, but in tabular form.

Beverage	Liking
A	6.4
B	7.3
C	6.8
D	7.1

Liking of four beverages on a 9 point scale

Figure 19.2: How four beverages score on overall liking, on a 9-point hedonic scale

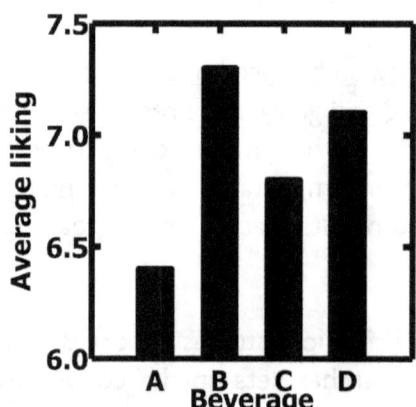

It's pretty easy to understand the data in both figure and table formats. It's a toss-up whether to use the figure or the table. In fact, it's really a matter of your personal preference.

<u>What do you do with lots and lots and lots of data?</u>

If you are going to limit yourself to data from three or four different beverages, or other stimuli, then it really doesn't matter whether you use tables or graphs. However, that's often not the case. In many research projects, there are lots of data to be presented. What should you do?

Rather than presenting a simple answer, good for all situations, approach the problem in a systematic way, by asking some questions about the data, about what you are trying to show, and just as importantly, to whom you are showing the data. What is the nature of the data? Are the data somehow connected, such as responses to different levels of salt in soup? Or are the data responses to different, unconnected stimuli?

When the data points are 'logically' connected, such as responses to different levels of salt, or some other 'continuum', then the truth of the matter is that you are interested in the pattern of the data. That is, you want to plot the data and see the slope of the line relating the rating (Y axis) to the stimulus level (X axis). So, when there is a natural relation between variables, it's probably best to show the data graphically by plotting the results. Even if the data are 'noisy', the plot shows the underlying relation. That's why statistical packages have curve fitting programs with two and three dimensional plots, like you see in Figure 19.1.

Now change the game. What happens when you deal with lots of data points, with each data point being important? It's one thing to talk about four beverages and put the results in a table. And, in that same vein, it's easy to plot dozens of data points when there are two variables, logically connected to each other. But what happens when you have meaningful data, where each point represents a relevant stimulus? Certainly there is no simply X-Y scatterplot, because the data aren't of that type. What do you do?

Let's move now to a more complex but quite realistic case, where you have data from a study. In the experiment, respondents rated a series of concepts, using a 0-100 interest scale. Each concept comprised 2-4 phrases. From the ratings, researchers were able to figure out the contribution of every element to the rating.

It's not our purpose to go into the details of the actual experiment. However, it is important to know how to present the data to the reader. This is part of your education. So, without further ado, here is the problem the researcher faces:

They have 16 different elements. What's the better way to show these elements- by table (see Table 19.2), or by graph (see Figure 19.3)? This isn't a book on the visual representation of data, for which you ought to see Edward Tufte's books (i.e., Tufte, 1982) on presenting information graphically. There are many problems that you may face when it comes time to writing your own papers. It's easy when you deal with simple problems such as how tasty is a well known beverage. The issue becomes substantially harder when your work involves a significant amount of information, with each piece of the information adding to the overall picture and, thus, of interest in and of itself.

This section was not put into this book simply to fill it with more and more examples, but rather to share with you an ongoing problem in scientific publishing on which you can cut your teeth.

So, before we end this section, the question remains for you to answer..which is the better representation of this data – the numbers (Table 19.2), or the graph (Figure 19.3)? First the table.

Table 19.2: How 16 phrases that one could say about a product drive the perception of the product as belonging to the 'High End' (just below luxury)

		Baseline perception of High End	32
Innovation Factor	A1	With functional features that anticipate what you want	6
	A2	With technological features that anticipate what you want	6
	A3	Innovative in continuity with the earlier generation of the same product	5
	A4	A natural extension of the current offer from its maker	3
Revolution ary factor	B4	Completely changes the way you live	9
	B1	Totally revolutionary	7
	B3	Just creates a new product category	0
	B2	Somewhat provocative	-2
Partnershi p factor	C2	Offers multiple functions	8
	C3	Combines benefits from different industries	7
	C1	Intuitive to use	6
	C4	Created thanks to a 'maverick CEO'	3
Thought leadership factor	D3	Comes from an authority I trust	2
	D2	One of the many creations of a public leader	-4
	D1	From an executive who is a public personality	-7
	D4	From a creator with a seducing charisma	-7

Source: Gofman, A., Bevolo, M., Moskowitz, H. 2009. Impact of Corporate Leadership and Innovation on Consumer Perception of Premium Products. XX Annual ISPIM Conference "The Future of Innovation" in Vienna, Austria. In Book of Abstracts of XX ISPIM Annual Conference

The data could be presented in the form of a graph or figure, such as Figure 19.3. Here, there is no plotting out of a 'curve' to show the relation among variables. Rather, the figure is a visual aid to help readers understand the numbers. Rather than having a table filled with data, it presents the same data in a picture.

Figure 19.3: Plot of Ideamap® data

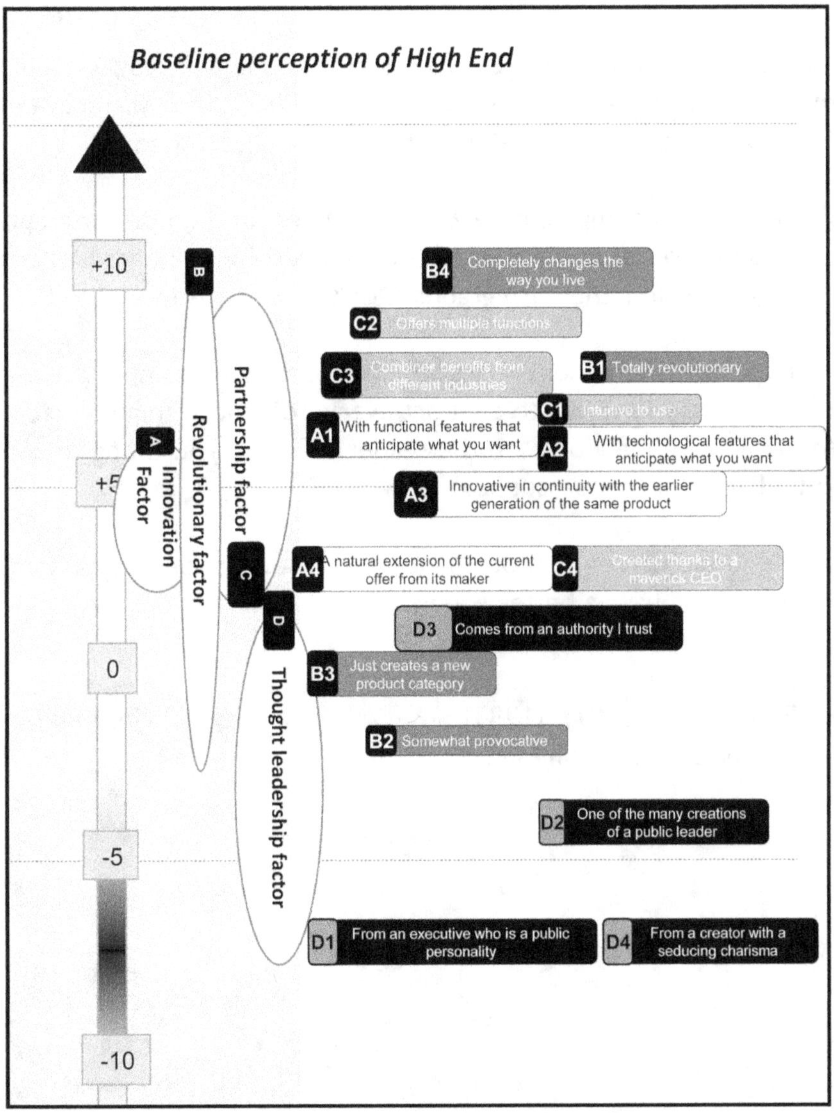

The bottom line is that you're not important enough – write to be read, not quoted

Let's go back to the basics. What are we really talking about? This is a chapter about presenting what you found. So, what then are the things you might think about?

1. Don't write magisterially. You're not ready to be great. Try to be adequate.

2. Try to write so that people will read your paper. More than likely, your paper is going to end up in the pile of papers, hundreds, thousands, millions even, that comprise the essence of science.

3. Keep to the point. Write simply, for the reader, not for the generations to come.

4. Write so that your point gets across. Do the mother test; write it so that your mother understands. If your mother has a Ph. D., then you may be out of luck. Find someone else to stand in place of your Dr. Mother.

5. Present the data appropriately. Don't waste time on pretty graphs if you can use tables. Conversely, if your tables don't get the point across because it's patterns you're after, then use graphs. Don't go crazy, however.

6. Think about the reader's reaction. Are you trying to impress with a mountain of data? Are you trying to support every point with minute statistical analysis (nothing could be worse on the reader)? Or are you trying to convince, present a logical discourse, supported by data?

7. Think about writing without data and without graphs. If you can do it, most likely you will have a better paper.

Bibliographic reference

Tufte, Edward R. (2001) [1983]. *The Visual Display of Quantitative Information* (2nd ed.). Cheshire, CT: Graphics Press.

CHAPTER 20

DEALING WITH REVIEWS, REVIEWERS, EDITORS, AND OTHER ASSORTED SHENANIGANS

<u>Introduction</u>

Talk to anyone who has been in the writing and publications 'game' for some time, and you're bound to hear about reviewers, reviews, editors, and the 'silliness' of journals. Of course, the word 'silliness' would not necessarily come up in conversation. That word is simply too bland, not sufficiently cutting, and certainly not able to convey the anger, fury, and immense disappointments which occur in the review process.

Our system of science in particular, but in academic research as a whole, is founded on a presumably wonderful thing called peer review. In its purest form, peer review is designed to be a self-correcting system. Presumably articles submitted for publication should not appear in the journals unless they are approved by colleagues who are in some way familiar with the topic area.

And so, begins the problem. When you think of science as an outsider, you probably have some stereotypical image of a person or group as '*earnest enquirers after the truth*'. Scienctists and other researchers are presumed to work because of nobler motives, such as the advancement of knowledge and, perhaps, in some cases, the greater common good. After all, goes the typical refrain, where would we be if science had not brought us technology to clothe and shelter us, to protect us from disease, to feed (and overfeed) us? So, scientists must, at the heart of it all, be good people because it is through science that we live better lives.

<u>How does peer review happen, and WiiFM (what's in it for me)</u>

When you are asked to review a paper, chances are the person who asks considers you to be a professional, either established or budding. A lot of us who went through graduate school got our first taste of professional life by being asked by a professor with whom we worked to review a paper. If you are like we were, you relished that first invitation. It was a sense that you were on your way to arriving.

Of course, reviewing is not writing a paper. For the most part, you are unrecognized. In fact, the review process prides itself on a 'blind review'. That is, the reviewer may know the author, but the author does not know the reviewer.

Armed with the charge to review the paper, you bustle off, and go through the paper microscopically. You look for inconstancies, incorrect statistics (a real forte of graduate students eager to prove themselves) and, at the end, you come back to your professor with a long paper, perhaps as long as the original submitted manuscript, filled with your notes, comments, and your valiant efforts to make this paper confirm to the tenets and mores of science that reside perhaps only in your own mind. That is, you rip the paper to shreds, not so much to help the authors as to prove on the first of your jousting fields that you are every bit a professional as the author of the paper.

By the time you finish your first review, you will recognize what a wonderful job you've done. It felt good to pore over someone else's work, perhaps as much for the sheer delight of being a voyeur, a fly on the wall, as it did for furthering science. No doubt you weighed your words; should you be super-critical and show off how much YOU know, or should you be modest and docile, in the role of the ever-dutiful graduate student? A hard choice, of course, but in the end your innate wisdom won. You did what you tought would put you in the best light with your professor or colleague. And, of course, to hell with the paper, which was just a vehicle. It was just a job. As Shakespeare said, which applies here so well, *He jests at scars that never felt a wound* (Romeo & Juliet, Act 2, Scene 2).

As you get more experience, both in your profession and in reviewing papers, your initial assiduousness will fade. That momentary first rapture of being asked to review a paper and, thus being implicitly accepted as an adult professional, will fade into the feeling of 'yet another paper to review'. You become the favorite reviewer of everyone, not so much because you are so developed and respected in your profession but because, in the end, peer review is a hygienic process, developed so that professionals can maintain the standards of their field.

Over time, what was fun may become onerous. When you're a graduate student, you do every one of the reviews with the same professional thoroughness. However, once you've been 'out' for a few years, no longer a newly-minted professional, you won't apply as much effort. And, finally, when you've been in the field for decades and have seen it all, your reviews will likely no longer be as meticulous, but more guiding and kinder, showing how the papers can be significantly improved, rather than grading each small peccadillo of the author(s). Finally, when your reviews are kind, you will be filled with compassion for the authors, with an understanding of their minds and hopes for the paper as you read between the lines. Then, you will have arrived to where peer review really should begin. You will no longer be grading others, shielded by the 'blind review process' where you can see but the authors cannot. Rather, you will now move others along in your reviews. You will have arrived.

Papers never really die

This section should be prefaced with a disclaimer or, perhaps, the very opposite of a disclaimer. The author has been closely associated with scientific journals, including founding journals (from the bottom up) as well as, of course, acting as so-called blind reviewer for articles submitted to a variety of disciplines. So, at some level, this section presents an insider's perspective on the review process.

We begin with the way the review process is constructed and practiced. In any field of science or, indeed, creative human endeavor, there are a limited number of individuals who can be considered the 'core group'. We're not talking about cliques, about who is friendly with whom, but rather individuals who are recognized as being conversant with the science. These individuals do not have to be well recognized or even famous researchers. Not at all. The individuals just have to know the topic matter. Indeed, quite often professors nominate students to be these experts.

When the editor of a journal gets a paper to review, it is the his/her job to decide whether or not the paper is even appropriate for the journal. It's surprising how many papers are submitted to journals by people whose topic is clearly not appropriate for the subject journal. This lack of fit is not altogether accidental. Of course, there are those who simply submit the paper to the wrong journal. We're all human and, sometimes, it's a matter of judgment. More frequently, however, papers rejected from one journal are reworked a bit and sent to another journal that seems more or less appropriate for the topic. There is often a lack of fit between those reworked papers, which may be inappropriate, and the new journal. It happens.

Enter the peer review process, which mostly works, but not always

In the grand scheme of things, the peer review process works reasonably well. That is, people's papers get reviewed, get improved, get out into the literature, and all too often, get forgotten over time. It's the natural course of life. Peer review has a great deal to do with it. Like rocks grinding against each other, eventually the rough edges get polished in the review process. Writing that's absolutely wrong typically gets weeded out, if not from the first article, then from the failure of the error to reappear in subsequent journals, with other editors and reviewers.

There are, however, problems with peer review. The system isn't perfect. Often, the reviewer is a direct competitor of the author(s); it can't be helped. There are a limited number of professionals in the industry conversant with any research topic. These are the reviewers. At the same time, these individuals are competitors to each other or, perhaps, professionally related (teacher/student). And so, the reviewer has a difficult time being truly impartial, and the process doesn't work as well.

These issues with peer review actually exist. They exist because it's the nature of individuals to be biased, no matter what their editor instructs, or what their conscience dictates in moments of quietude and reflection. Of course, one could be a saint, recognizing the temptations, and then working mightily to overcome them, being fair in the review, indeed, leaning over. This is judging on the scales of righteousness, as the *Ethics of the Fathers* might adjure us. But, reality is far different and, perhaps, more like that of St. Augustine, who said '*Oh Lord save me, but not yet*'.

Peer review problems occur most frequently when reviewers hold different opinions from that of the author(s) or, even more venally, when reviewers have conducted research of a similar type and want to get 'into print' more quickly. This ethical bind occurs far more frequently than one is willing to admit. It troubles the ethical reviewers. The results of the quandry damage the soul of the reviewer (yes, the soul), the person whose work is being reviewed, and the field of science.

The dynamic duo

Whenever there is creative work being judged, human emotions enter the fray. And, in the case of peer review, we end up with this dynamic duo, forever partnering with each other in their dance from hell:

The problem reviewer: In a sense, the reviewer is compromising his integrity. In order to suppress the submission, the reviewer acts unfairly, perhaps not conscious of it at all. However, the emotions are there, the desire to suppress the paper and, perhaps, even latent hostility towards the author submitting the paper. For the most part, the hostility is not so latent. One can read the hostility rather directly, through the snide comments, through the direct allegations about the competence of the research and, indirectly, of the researcher. In the end, it is the reviewer, using the protocol and the protection of blind review, who lashes out at the author in many ways, betraying anger when professional detachment and intellectual honesty are called for. This behavior is all too common. Most scientists have encountered such *ad hominen* reviews for papers that were, at worst, mediocre and, at best, breakthrough but would cast competitor scientists into a slight shadow.

The problem author: We all want to be loved; a few of us really deserved to be loved, especially by our colleagues. The problem author is one who believes that a critical review is an insult to one's *amour propre*, one's standing in the profession, one's future. The problem author is one who fights back, not judiciously, in a measured way, but in an ongoing rebuttal. The problem author is one who will not modify something, who stands (undeservedly) proud, believing that his/her paper is above reproach. The problem author is the flip side of the problem reviewer. The problem reviewer wants to destroy someone else in order to build himself up, while the problem author wants to protect and deny to maintain whatever edifice has been constructed, deserved or not. The response of the problem author is rebuttal of every point made by the reviewer, sometimes in a rationale way, sometimes as mere dismissal.

Dealing with reviews and winning

Keep your eye on the goal, which is to get the paper published. Period. Nothing else. Except for out and out rejection by reviewers, reinforced by the editor (or even a so-called immediate desk-rejection by the editor), there's always hope for getting one's manuscript published. A lot depends upon the author's mental state. When each of the reviewer's points can be addressed, either with a modest rebuttal or a change, there is hope for the paper. A good strategy recognizes that most reviewers will accept some rebuttals as long as a reasonable number of the review points are addressed. It's always good form to make the changes, and then show these chances in a modest fashion. Here is one approach:

1. In the actual reviewer form, containing the text of the review, color the reviewer's points so that the individual points stand out. A good color for this is yellow shade.

2. Then, in a different shade, put in your answer. This can be simply the word 'done', or 'done, with the following specifics'. That section should be shaded in a different color (i.e., green) and indented, to set it off from the yellow-shaded comment from the reviewer. Be short and sweet in this section, unless you have to defend a specific viewpoint. In that case, you should marshal your arguments and present them in a respectful way.

3. Finally, when the reviewer's point has resulted in a change in the text, copy/paste that section of the text just below the answer to the reviewer (#2 above). Skip a line, paste in the section, put the section in bold and italics, and drop the size of the letter by 2 units or so (i.e., so a Times New Roman 12 would be now italicized, dropped to a Times New Roman 10, and then shaded in green).

4. Following the preceding three steps, accept and rewrite according to the reviewer's critique, pointing out what you did in concrete, non-confrontational terms. It's likely that the paper will be accepted on the next review. You, the author, will have clearly addressed the issues and, furthermore, even the most problematical reviewer will have no recourse but to accept the paper.

Computerization efficiency and the production–line mentality

Despite the belief that reviewers have power and, perhaps, a perverted streak of sadism or at least untrammeled curiosity, the truth of the matter is much different. For the most part, reviewers are not particularly interested. You may be; they're just not. Most reviewers are busy with their own lives, whether chasing grants to fund their research, teaching, or just doing other things. There isn't sufficient emotional reward in editing other people's manuscripts, unless one gets to edit the manuscript of a friend or an enemy and, by happenstance, one is still in the state of active emotional response rather that having passed to a mature equanimity.

By the time one reaches middle age, and certainly older, one has reviewed enough manuscripts to be fair, to uncover and praise the good and not just excoriate the weak in a manuscript. In a word, one's ready to do the job for which peer review was originally designed. It's then that the problems arise, but problems of a different type, as we see below.

The big problem for an editor is to get reviewers who actually will do what they promised. It used to be, a decade or more ago, that editors would write personalized notes atop form letters, asking the reviewer to look over a manuscript. The letter was somewhat personalized and so, in the typical case, a reviewer felt a personal obligation to the editor to review the paper. The editor would, on occasion, find that a particular reviewer was tardy and either call the reviewer with whom he/she had a personal acquaintance, or more likely, craft a nice letter, and send it out.

Publishing, specifically of edited journals, demands that reviewers adhere to their promised schedules, of 30 days in the standard case. Publishing companies such as Elsevier, responsible for hundreds of journals, have made it their business to become increasingly efficient through computerization. So, a manuscript comes to the editor, often submitted electronically through a website, in the form of a Word document which is automatically converted to an Adobe pdf file. The editor then selects a few reviewers, clicks on the right button, and an electronic request is sent to each reviewer. After the reviewer accepts, all that needs to be done is for her/him to click on the link embedded in the email.

Acceptance by clicking on the link sets into motion steps that makes the review both efficient and impersonal. Indeed, the impersonal aspect is so great as to make the review process seem like a clinical test. The reviewer, having accepted the assignment, clicks on the embedded link, which sends the reviewer to a personal or micro-site, for that reviewer alone. The site contains 'tasks for the reviewer', although the word 'task' may be changed to something less mechanical. The reviewer can download the manuscript or read it online.

<u>Shenanigans in reviewer land – what happens when a reviewer disappears?</u>
It may sound strange and irresponsible, but reviewers do disappear. The editor will receive an agreement that the reviewer will assess a manuscript. All the paperwork, which today is principally through e-mail, notifies the reviewer of the deadline for the journal to receive the review. Today's technology makes it even easier for the reviewer to live up to the deadline, because everything has been automated and computerized. The reviewer need only read the manuscript and make the necessary comments.

So… what happens? The inevitable, of course. Reviewers disappear. The editor has to round up the reviewers, remind them that their papers are due, cajole them.

Finally, most of the laggard reviewers return their reviews a bit chastened, of course, but dutifully. Some reviewers entirely disappear, plunging the editor into a quandary. Should the editor use the reviews that have come in or should the editor invite new reviewers? In either case, the outcome is unfair to the author unless, of course, the newly invited reviewer is more positive toward the manuscript than the disappearing reviewer would have been.

What typically happens in these situations is that the author waits and waits. Eventually, the system corrects itself. The missing reviewer either is rounded up to complete the task, rounded up and then begs off to be replaced by someone else, or entirely ignored, with the decision taken on the basis of the reviews in hand.

This is not to suggest that missing reviewers is a common occurrence. Late reviews are the rule, but not missing reviewers. They constitute a professional slap in the face, primarily towards the editor, but possibly a passive aggressive response to an author, whom the missing reviewer dislikes. In any event, missing reviewers are out of bounds, improper, and 'lose points' professionally, at least in the mind of the editor. The missing review may succeed, however, in torpedoing the paper without ever having to go on record as doing so. It's not a nice ploy, and should be discouraged. Perhaps, whipping missing reviewers in public or posting a list of them on a website would work. However, no professional wants to risk that. In the case of irresponsible reviewers it's better to let the authors drown than to lose the respect, cooperation, and the protection of unspoken non-aggression pacts with other professionals in the field. Here, *realpolitik* rides again, at the expense of the hapless author. *C'est la vie – if you can't stand the heat, then get out of the kitchen.*

<u>What do you do when you know the editor will desk reject you</u>

Desk rejection refers to the unpleasant situation where the journal editor immediately rejects your paper for any of a number of different reasons. The reason most typically given is that the paper '*does not fit*'. However, all too often, desk rejection is used as a way to ensure that a paper does not get published. Harsh as it may seem, editors are not above moral corruption and are tempted to use their positions as a way to quash papers of individuals who are perceived as threats. This malicious behavior, while not particularly common, occurs from time to time. The editors need not give a reason behind their desk rejections, but often they do by saying that the paper '*simply does not fit this journal…good luck to you in your quest to publish this no-doubt important paper (but..nimj..not in MY journal you don't)*'.

Is there anything that you can do? The answer is no and yes. No, you cannot get the paper published in that journal. Desk rejections are fairly brusque affairs, usually handled with absolute indifference. By the time a paper is desk rejected, there is very little that an author can do because the editor has the final authority. The 'game' cannot be taken to a higher level, since no one is willing to fight the editor. It just isn't worth it.

Perhaps the best strategy in the case of desk rejection is to lick one's wounds, modify the paper, and submit it somewhere else. Indeed, nothing succeeds in salving the wound as getting an acceptance somewhere else. And, it's always a great pleasure to tell the editor who rejected the paper how wise the decision was, because it allowed you to improve the paper and publish it in a 'more appropriate journal'. Short of kicking the editor in the shins, or some other hostile act, this is about the most you can do. And, in the long run, it's the best you can do. Don't get mad, get published.

☆ ☆ ☆

CHAPTER 21

AVOID GETTING HIGH JACKED DURING YOUR PRESENTATION

It's the same story again and again, the presentation to a thousand faces, but really one face. You work very hard on your study. You analyze the data. Nothing is left to chance. Nothing at all. You stay up all night rehearsing. For every question you can possibly be asked, you have an answer. You do something you haven't done for 10 years – write all your notes on small index cards, those little 3" x 5" cards that you used when you took notes. The cards are small so you can shuffle them around. Now, you're using them, not because you need to, but because they make you feel comfortable. And that's what's important right now.

The big moment has just arrived or, perhaps, will at any second now. You'll walk into the conference room, maybe even one of those modern, high-tech rooms featuring a camera because your presentation is going to be presented on a web conference, or broadcast live to some remote areas of the world. You're comfortable in your position at the head of the table. Of course, you're a little nervous. But, then again, you're the master of the data, the master of this presentation. It will be what YOU choose to tell people that will make the difference. You know they'll be interested. Whether it's your Ph.D. defense or, perhaps, reporting on a study you ran in a business meeting, or presenting your data at a conference to your colleagues; in any event, you're in charge.

Exciting, isn't it? Of course it's exciting. After all, what could possibly go wrong? Sure you're a little nervous, but that's par for the course.

<u>The devil in the blue (dress, suit, jacket)</u>

> But, Mousie, thou art <u>no</u> thy lane,
> In proving foresight may be vain;
> The best-laid schemes <u>o'</u> mice <u>an</u> 'men
> <u>Gang</u> <u>aft</u> agley,
> An'lea'e us nought <u>but</u> grief an' pain,
> For promis'd joy!
> (Robert Burns, 'To a mouse')

Scottish poet Robert Burns had it right when he wrote those lines which, incidentally, mean that the best laid plans often go awry. And, you would be correct in thinking that this happens in meetings. We're not going to talk about giving a bad presentation, messing up one's presentation with the wrong materials, and essentially screwing things up oneself. We've dealt with that. We're going to talk about something far more insidious, very common, and positively destructive when it happens.

Let's go back to the presentation. You're at the presentation, pretty well prepared. The presentation is going smoothly like it should since, after all, you know your material, and you, not the others, are the master of what you have done. The meeting you're having is to present results, so the spirit of the meeting is one of communication.

As you move along in your presentation you're feeling increasingly relaxed. The audience seems to be getting it although, of course, you can't get into the minds of the people sitting listening. But, for the most part, their body language tells you that they understand. There aren't any people sitting with their hands folded so tightly across their chests that any additional pressure is likely to break a rib.

And then, it happens. From the back of the room, perhaps from one of the seats against the wall rather than from one around the table where the real players are, you see a hand shoot up. The hand is not a diffident hand. The smile on the face makes you feel a bit queasy and you have a sense that something is about to change, that you're going to be dealing with something new.

> *'Your presentation is interesting..but..it's probably invalid because you didn't
> ….(add your own language here)*

Usually, the high jacking doesn't begin with a head-on attack but with a slight compliment, damning with faint praise. Then there is the tip-off….the word 'invalid' or any of a dozen other words. Statisticians like to use the word 'invalid' when they are about to high jack a presentation. Market researchers will have 'issues' or 'concerns', especially if the researchers came from the advertising agency. Management with bottom-line responsibility, such as marketers or general managers, don't usually high jack meetings, so you won't hear any of this nonsense 'issues', 'concerns', 'problems', or 'invalidity' from their mouths, unless they perceive errors that are so egregious as to actually call into question what you're saying.

<u>What really just happened?</u>
You, the readers of this book, who are students, young professionals and scientists, should understand that the scenario we just discussed is not a normal, everyday interchange among serious seekers of the truth. If you have had experience in scientific meetings, in student-professor interchanges, in debates with your fellow students about almost anything, you can probably tell when someone is honestly critiquing what you are doing, or holds a different point of view. The feeling that the other person is 'playing fair with you' comes through. You may not like what the other person is saying, and you may feel terribly irritated that someone could hold such a 'stupid point of view', but you don't get a sense of dishonesty, a gnawing feeling of disingenuousness.

You may get sense of dishonesty, that something's not right, however, in one of these meetings where the question doesn't seem 'right', doesn't seem 'on target'. You may get a feeling that the person who just asked the question is trying to steer the presentation in a different direction. And, often, you'll be correct.

Let's dissect this interaction a little bit more, to understand some motives of the person who just asked the question, that individual who may have tried to high jack the meeting. We may or may not be correct. The question may be honest. Let's see some things that the individual might say in the course of questioning your presentation, talk about what these statements mean, and then present ideas about how to defend against them. The reason for doing so is very simple.

> *A person who high jacks your presentation can destroy your reputation in public and cause significant amounts of damage to you for years to come. Furthermore, the high jacking need not remain in public where you can defend against it. High jacking can continue behind the scenes and turn into professional slander. Do not underestimate its seriousness.*

> *On the other hand, not all high jacking is evil. Some is great, good entertainment.*

High jacking scenario #1 – Irrelevant but fear-inducing statistical 'issues'

Statisticians specialize in the numerical analysis of data. If truth be told, most marketers, product developers, and consumer researchers are not comfortable with statistical methods, because they are difficult to understand and often presented in ways that make them remote rather than available. Furthermore, statisticians have always held themselves a breed apart, both working for their 'clients' the researchers, but also fellows in a professional brotherhood that occasionally evolves into a priesthood. Of course, not all statisticians are this way and, perhaps, just a few. But that few suffice to tarnish the entire profession.

The statistician sitting in the meeting can high jack by raising a variety of tangential questions, some more insidious than others. The simplest high jack, which is probably not really a high jack, is a question about the statistics that are used to analyze the result. When the question is comprehensible to the others in the room, such as the marketers, and when it can be answered in a sentence or two, allowing you to get back to the topic, then it's a fair question, although a disconcerting one, but fair, nonetheless.

The real high jack comes when the statistician introduces a notion that seems utterly alien and yet frightening, a notion that the entire study suffers from an irreparable fault. For example, in the 1970's and 1980's, a number of statisticians sitting in various meetings asked these questions, prefaced by intimations that if the data did not have these properties, the entire study was invalid.

1. The raw data distribution had 'fat tails', and was not normally distributed.

2. The interactions were not properly designed.

3. The mathematical models were inappropriate.

It's not that questions high jack a meeting. Rather, it's the fact that the issues involved do not pertain to any of the actual problems for which the study was designed. That is, the statistician is attempting to change the focus from the actual project, to a venue where only the statistician has the competence to judge the validity of the results. When one of these questions or something like them is raised at a meeting, and the response is a quizzical and somewhat fearful look by the marketing client in the room, there is an attempted high jacking going on. Rather than addressing the substantive issue, the high jacker diverts it to a statistical one, leaving both the marketing and product developers dumbfounded, in the dark.

A most effective way to deal with high jacking is the simple response '*That's a good question, we'll address it later, at the end of the meeting, or off-line*'. You haven't acted defensively, but have simply said that 'we'll put the question on hold and keep going with the substantive part of the presentation'. The statistician will be satisfied or, at least, blocked during the high jacking attempt. You may return to the question at the end of the meeting, but most likely not. The question was irrelevant from the get-go and, eventually, during the course of your presentation you and everyone else will have forgotten about it. The statistician will not be particularly interested in pursuing the actual answer at the end of the meeting, since the issue wasn't of interest anyway. It was the high jacking that was the objective, not the answer to the question.

Although we have dealt with this simple case in detail, and shown how to resolve it, do not by any means underestimate the deadliness of statistical high jacking. It has destroyed more meetings and embarrassed more people than you might guess. It is effective; a naked struggle for the high jacker to be known, become important, even for a moment, but at your expense.

Don't let it happen. Never let the high jacking go on for more than 15 seconds. Stay with the topic, even if you feel that you are being rude. No one cares about the high jacker's question. Period.

High jacking scenario #2 – Conferences - The 'paper' within the question

Some years ago, before the advent of PowerPoint presentations there was a world of scientific meetings characterized by the ubiquitous 2x2 slide. These cardboard bordered slides would have to be inserted deftly into the round Kodak projector tray that can hold up to 200 slides. It was a tedious affair to set up one's slides, go through them, and then hand the slide carousel back to the projectionist, but of course everyone giving a paper had to master that skill. And, by the way, very rarely did anyone use all 200 slots, because almost nobody would have enough time to present all the slides.

With this scene in mind, you should realize that having the slides easily loaded meant that an adept member of the audience could, upon asking a question during the question and answer period, request permission of the speaker and the projectionist to 'show a slide or two'. And that's how it started.

Like the plane with the door to the cockpit unlocked, just inviting a highjack, so we have the scientific meeting. You see, the projectionist was sitting in the audience with the projector unprotected. The savvy high jacker at the scientific meeting would begin as follows:

> "I have a simple question. (makes a statement). To back up my question, I happen to have a few slides of data that will make the question clearer. (walks over to the projector, gently takes control of the projector tray to the astonishment of the projectionist, loads a few slides), and begins to deliver a 'paper within a paper'".

To watch this adroit, adept, almost exquisitely executed maneuver was exciting. Indeed, many in the audience knew what was happening. The *'paper within the paper'* never damaged the speaker; not really. It wasn't the high jacking of a business meeting as was the case with the statistical high jack, which sought to undermine the presentation by appealing to statistical esoterica, intimidating the marketer more than helping the project. Rather, it was some individual, usually well known, middle age or older, who felt he or she simply had to share his data with the audience. It was more like the cuckoo bird than the wasp. The cuckoo bird lays its eggs in another bird's nest, so that the host bird raises the young. There's no assassination, no bad will, no raising of the audience's anxiety level, just high jacking to get one's ideas across. The wasp, in contrast, lays its eggs in the body of the host, say a caterpillar. The young wasps come out and devour the living host.

Now as to prevention. It's hard to prevent this second, good-natured high jacking because it's conducted and because the high jacker seizes control of the slide carousel, inserts his slides, and projects his data as he makes his 'presentation within a presentation'. And it's done in good fun and spirits. There aren't any bad feelings.

Unfortunately, technology is making this high jacking a thing of the past. Now that we have computers with PowerPoint ® presentations, with the projection crew out of range of the high jacker, we don't see these wonderfully amusing events any more. They're a delight to talk about, just great good fun.

Summing up

There are two ways to high jack a meeting, one more fun, the other more lethal, which leave bad feelings for a lifetime. The former, the fun high jack, occurs when an academic upstages the presenter, in essence by giving a 'paper or talk within a talk'. The typical way is through asking a question, which allows the high jacker to present a set of slides. Most of the audience who watches these antics know exactly what's happening. It's in good fun. The high jacker may be serious, but for the most part, even the high jacked presenter ends up smiling. A well-done high jack of a paper, with good spirit and in the honest scientific tradition, is a joy to watch. It's a work of art, the well-done artful dodge. And, as you may feel, when reading this description, the academic paper high jack is quickly forgotten, with very few hard feelings.

On the other hand, there is the deadly serious high jack, conducted by statisticians or occasionally by others, who want to cast real doubts on the true validity of the data. In so doing, they make every attempt to impugn the researcher. Make no mistake. This type of high jacking is not meant as a serious question to get at the truth. This high jacking is done in devious ways, to regain territory that seems to be ceded to the presenter. This sort of high jacking leaves reputations damaged and creates ill will, often lasting a lifetime. There is no fun here. The is simply maliciousness or, at least, a desire by the high jacker to show that his job is relevant, he is relevant, even if it means throwing a random monkey wrench into the entire works, and bringing into undeserved doubt on a perfectly good research project that has already been completed. And, in contrast to the former good-feelings, this serious high jack ends in bad feelings, when attendees and presenters realize that the meeting has been high jacked. No one wins here, especially not the company.

✲ ✲ ✲

CHAPTER 22

WHAT YOU WRITE AND HOW YOU WRITE – MIRRORING YOUR CAREER

<u>Introduction</u>

In this book, a great deal of emphasis has been made about writing. Writing, for a professional, produces a record of one's life. Inevitably, when you write, your work product turns out to record your life. You try as you will, to follow the dictates of science, be objective, couch your language in a dense, passive, or third person tone, with the air of formal science. Nevertheless, there will always be some of YOU which sneaks in.

So, rather than trying to dissect what makes good professional writing, let's have a bit of fun in this chapter. Let's dissect the writer as s/he goes through life. All writers differ from each other. Here, we will only focus on a limited domain of writers, this author (me). This section will be autobiographical, dealing with how I look at what I've written over 40 years. This journey to self-knowledge, perhaps a bit egotistical to you, is absolutely fascinating to me. Since I'm doing the writing, I'll continue along this path. However, please feel free to skip this chapter.

<u>Learning to write - Smitty</u>

When we young, unformed students arrived at Harvard in the middle 1960's, we all had reasonable backgrounds. None of us was illiterate. The Graduate Record Examinations had required a sample of our writing. We had read psychology, were familiar with the great books of English literature and, in general, considered ourselves fairly well educated.

When you read, you think you can write. And, of course, when you're really educated, say having read poetry and history, Keats, Shelley, Byron, Gibbon, you have that distinct feeling that just by being exposed to the great stylists, the great authors, that you, too, can write easily. Harvard, and especially Smitty (S.S.) Stevens and Dick (Richard) Herrnstein, quickly disabused us of those self-delusions! Yes, perhaps, we were chosen because the admissions committee for the Psychology Department saw promise in us. However, that promise had to be honed by work; writing was that work.

Smitty's point of view concerning writing can be summed up by a little story, which he delighted in telling during one of his editorial sessions. These sessions lasted an hour or two, during which time Smitty would carefully go over every sentence. It didn't matter whether the topic was drivel. It was the sentence structure. And, somewhere in the middle or, really, a bit after the middle, when Smitty was in his best form, he'd come out with the following:

> *You know…my aunt would ask me.. "Smitty, what DO YOU DO at Harvard?"*
> *And I would tell her, (Voice gets deeper and louder) " I TEACH WRITING."*

I make light of it now, forty five years later. Yet, the truth of the matter is that the exercise of writing, sitting face to face with a piece of paper that will not go away, is a powerful way to learn how to think. If you can't write about it, you don't know it. And, if you can't communicate it, you still don't know it. Because, as Smitty would say, if you know it, then you should be able to communicate it to HIS aunt. Period.

You write 'where' you are

Now, looking back over these decades, it's become clear that there is no one way of scientific writing. There are many types of scientific writings. These writings co-vary with age. Let's see how. A word of caution here. The opinions expressed in this section and, indeed, of every other section of this book, are those of the author and not of the publisher.

Somewhere along the line, we're 'taught' that good scientific writing is concise, formal, follows a strict choreography, and is meant to last for the ages as establishing some fact, some insight about the way 'nature works'. If the prescription for scientific writing is not exactly that, it's some facsimile. The bottom line is that there is an established way.

You, we, almost anyone can recognize this formal style. The resulting papers are, for the most part, pretty unreadable. Oh, there are nuggets here and there, probably in the abstracts or, perhaps, in the conclusions. The papers do not, however, draw in the reader. Of course, that's not the intent of this sort of writing in the first place. The intent is to document, but in a way that is acceptable to the fraternity of fellow professionals.

And reading these papers? Well, perhaps the best that one could say is that it's good to be a young and patient graduate student, filled with energy, with a *tabula rasa* mind, and sufficient piss and vinegar to withstand the assault of such writing. Yes, the writing is archival and certainly documents what happened. Indeed, it could not document any better. Many of the results are punctuated with virtually unreadable interstices, statistical affirmation that the observation is 'statistically significant' (whatever that may mean). Reading these papers is like walking through a melting, ice covered sidewalk, a few days after the snow has ended. You know, when the ice has been packed down and then the temperature hits 50 degrees F. There are lots of holes in the ice, water just above the surface, with some splashing from the ongoing car. It's a thoroughly taxing and unpleasant experience. Of course, this description may seem a bit cruel, but it gets the point across. Writing should invite, not mortify the flesh of the mind.

Looking for patterns in people rather than patterns in nature

As I've gotten older, it's become clearer to me that the topic and way in which I write speak more to my age than I could ever have imagined. When I was far younger, in the middle 1960's to the middle 1980's, corresponding to my mid 20's to mid 40's, my writing and, indeed, my conversation was future oriented. I spoke about the future, I wrote about patterns in nature and, in general, what I dealt with looked forward. My writing was all about me, understanding nature, about taking a stand and fighting to establish myself.

What about the writing of this period? Try reading your own reading from two decades ago, not so much for its content as to discover 'who' was actually writing. Reading the writing, I detect a younger man who was not particularly sensitive. He was more than ready to play the game of 'style' that was the *rule du jour*. In general, he was a less than self-aware researcher. The writing conformed almost perfectly to the demands of the scientific profession. And, if the writing was less than readable, was not particularly felicitous, it is clear that the writer of the papers, namely a younger me, was not particularly perturbed. In summary, work from decades ago was to the point. Which is to say that the work was/is appropriately scientific, hard to read and, most likely, irrelevant except as yet another micro-contribution to the not-particularly-readable literature of science.

The reasons underlying that type of writing, with its tight compactness are, in fact, simple. At that time, I was interested in establishing myself, making sure that I was a 'politically correct' part of the scientific establishment. And, of course, like all scientists interested in the approbation of my colleagues, I molded my writing to the demands of what the journals called 'appropriate scientific style' or some other such phrase. The important thing was to fit in, to play the game, to be like the others. The papers had to appear in high level, high impact, scientific journals. The form had to be appropriate. And the content? Well, as long as the form was OK and met with standards that would allow me to boast of yet another 'refereed paper in an A journal', the rest was irrelevant. It was the writing of a young person, imitating what he thought the true scientist was. It was a child playing adult. What a horrible thing to say about oneself, about one's motives, but not without grains of truth.

Moving on to today and even looking at this book as an example, I, and hopefully you, see something different. No, the discipline of science is not so apparent. There is no magical sequence of abstract, followed by a literature review to show that I'm conversant with the contributions of others and, thus, the paper fits into the stream of what has flowed before. Nor is there a mind-twisting methods section, where I proceed to dazzle by an artful combination of experimental method of virtually incomprehensible statistics. Nor are there the perfunctory sections on discussion, where I link the minor results from a minor experiment to the solution of many of the world's problems or a least to the solution of some major issues in the field upon which the paper touches, if ever so slightly.

None of the above. This book, like so many others of its type, as well as even shorter conference papers, reflect the writings of an older, seasoned, humanistic professional emerging from a life of science and fact. Facts are certainly important. They're the little rocks and stones, shattered pieces of brick, on which the road is created. But it's really the 'story', not the facts. The story is human-centered, not science and fact-centered. What's now of interest to me is 'why', more in the nature of 'why something happens', than 'why is it actually the way it is'. The objectivity and stultified approach of rigorous science has given way to the softer, less rigorous writing of the novelist, who is seeking motive in action, while looking at the human comedy through the story behind the research.

There is always a risk in following one's own desires and style. Scientists are often harsh judges, especially when you attack their professional demeanor, and their stylized writing and public presentation behavior. When it comes to me and my writing, many scientific colleagues and editors feel that it is simply too loose, too unorganized, more chatty, less august, and lacking the necessary gravitas.

When I first became aware that I was writing to be read rather than writing to be cited, I hoped that the writing style would not be a problem. But it remained a problem for years. And, over those years, I tried to write as a writer, not as a scientist. During the course of those years, it became increasingly obvious that to write the way everyone wanted, with gravitas and stiffness, might mean publication but it might just as well, and probably more likely, mean obscurity. And so, I chose writing that you could read, rather than writing that was a tight nodule inside an equally tight container. In other words, I chose to breathe, to exhale, to let out my girdle so to speak, rather than stay tightly made up in the corset of science. And, the laxity may have even helped. If you are reading these words, you will have at least gotten to here. And that, is what really matters.

Summing up

If you live long enough, you get old. And, if you get old, you change. And, if you change, you may well become a heretic. And, well, that's not so bad, not really bad at all.

Scientists are taught how to write up their scientific experiemnts. As I've said throughout the chapter and, probably alluded to throughout this book, science writing is in desperate need of a transfusion. Someone ought to tell that community that it's OK to write so that others can read it. Scientific papers need not be boring. They should tell the story, not just be a report of what happened.

What all this means is that in science there is room for, indeed a need for, this chimera called soul. Despite our attempts to be objective, to laying down the observations of how nature works, proclaiming our gravitas as professionals throughout the world, it's not such a bad idea to write so that other people read and, perhaps, actually even enjoy what we're writing. Oh happy day that someone could pick up a scientific paper and actually enjoy the science inside, well described, rather than reading the paper as one might read a legal document – checking little jot and title!

✧ ✧ ✧

CHAPTER 23

DO NOT LET THE PERFECT BE THE ENEMY OF THE GOOD

My late father, Moses Moskowitz of blessed memory, would often tell me the words cited as the title of this chapter. He was a descendent of Chassidic rabbis from the Galician province of Austrian Poland. As a child, father learned that perfection was really unobtainable. Although it was important to excel, or to work towards excelling, it was impossible to be perfect. After all, he knew, we were created as people, not as angels – no matter what our grandmothers may have said or thought!

The notion of the perfect being the enemy of good continues to be relevant. It is worth a chapter in itself. Rather than giving principles and suggestions, let's see what perfection misses, as well as what imperfection catches. We'll illustrate the value of not being perfect by talking about the history of a research technology called IdeaMap®.net , which allows researchers to understand what's important in the mind of consumers through systematically varying ideas or messages, combining them, presenting them to the consumer, getting reactions, and then deducing what elements drive the reactions.

You can learn a lot about a person by letting them respond to small combinations of ideas, such as the combination shown in figure 23.1. The method itself is not of interest. What *is* of interest to us is how clients respond when they, the clients, are presented with new approaches. The responses, not of consumers, but of professionals confronted with 'new' ideas, makes for interesting learning for anyone who wants to spend a career in an industry. And, you get to learn a lot about people!

Phrases about coffee

Figure 23.1: Example of a systematically varied set of phrases about coffee, combined into a single vignette or test concept. The test participant sees the combination on the computer screen, and rates the combination on a scale, such as 'interest in the coffee' (1=not at all interested ... 9 = extremely interested).

Rich, great taste
Share a precious quiet moments
with coffee and good friends

Learning by playing versus learning by systematized instruction

When my scientific market research firm introduced the IdeaMap®.net computer program in 1990, we were selling to two types of people. Both groups were professionals and both groups were employed. The differences between the groups had to be in their minds:

Group 1 consisted of individuals who needed structure and process. They wanted detailed manuals and would not work with the computer program unless everything was written out in detailed steps. These people were incapable of playing with programs, and had to be guided through them. None of them wanted to make a mistake. It was absolutely vital to them that the front to back path be specified, including examples of ideas to put in at the front end, as well as the expected results and interpretation at the back end. Needless to say, most of Group 1 never really adopted the IdeaMap®.net program. It was simply not set up for them to go through in a systematic way, with all the contingencies specified.

Group 2 people, however, were quite adventurous. Yes, this group wanted user manuals but, in reality, they wanted to play with the program. Some parts of the program were well explained and illustrated by the user manual, but other parts of the program were not explained at all. Nonetheless, this second group dove in, made alot of mistakes, but eventually got the 'hang' of it, and went on to use the program extensively, both in business research and in scientific studies.

What's interesting about these two groups is that both were truly interested in using the IdeaMap® .net technology to create better ideas. One group was able to learn by playing and, everntually, got really facile. They made mistakes, had fun, and they learned. The other group was unable to play, needed guidance, a set of specific instructions and, only then, would they feel comfortable. The first group wanted to be perfect, or at least error free; they learned slowly, or not at all. The second group didn't care about being perfect; so they learned quickly.

Applying the good-vs-perfect tradeoff to everyday life

How do we apply the idea of finding the 'good' without wasting precious minutes looking for the 'perfect'? And, in fact, should we settle for the good and not look for perfect? Ask a young woman, not yet married, who is looking for Mr. Right. She might well tell you that she's looking for the perfect man. Naturally, of course, she will add, for her. Now if this young lady were now suddenly transformed in front of our eyes to a middle-aged, unmarried woman, perhaps that dream of finding Mr. Perfect (or better Mr. Right) might well evolve in front of our eyes to finding Mr. Almost -OK.

So, to get down to business. The first thing we should observe is that the younger person, the new professional, carries around in his (or her) mind this notion of perfection, that work has to be perfect in order for one to make a major contribution. As you will have read before, that's just simply not the case, nor could it ever be the case. We judge ourselves by the accomplishments of professionals with many years of practice, or against the work of wunderkind geniuses, Mozarts of the different professions. Many of us feel that unless the work is of such caliber as theirs, it is simply not worth pursuing.

Nothing could be further from the truth. The reality is that most of the work that any of us do in our lifetimes is, at best, modest in its quality, temporary in influence and, ultimately, forgotten. Certainly, we will have inspired moments. But the vast majority of our work product will be average. If you don't believe that, try doing two simple observational experiments:

1. Go through the scientific literature of the most highly regarded journals in your field. Look at the papers and rate them as you personally perceive their importance. If you feel that you are biased because of the authors, who are all well regarded, try doing it double blind so you don't know the authors. Furthermore, should you want to escape the zeitgeist, look at journals that were published say 20 years ago.

2. Now do the same thing but for papers in a far less prestigious journal. Do the same exercise for papers of the same type. Again, score these papers on your perception of their importance and, perhaps, on other attributes.

3. If you are like the rest of us, you'll be surprised. The truth of the matter is that the papers in the highly reputed journals are about the same in perceived importance as the papers in the less reputable journals.

4. The reality is that the vast work product of science is really a compendium of information, dotted occasionally with important papers. Furthermore, the importance of these key papers may not be apparent to you or to your colleagues, or even to the profession at the time the papers are published. Years may have to go by before the paper is recognized as seminal.

<u>If a researcher's work product is destined to be just 'modest', then what should one strive for?</u>

What should be the goal of your work? If perfection is not attainable, then what?

What an important question. If you can't have perfection, then what should you do? Answering this question can take a lifetime, but you don't have a lifetime to practice. Should you only work on first order problems, or should you accept second order problems, which you can then solve and master? Or should you continue to work on first order problems, and be satisfied with what you can do, as long as it's your best work? These are pretty hard questions to answer.

It's important to realize that first order problems are always more interesting than second order ones. So, when you have a chance, work on the first order problems. You may not do as well or be the first, but at the end of your career, you won't feel that you have wasted precious minutes on what may turn out to be drivel.

Now, for the really tough question. How perfect should your efforts be? After all, you could spend years and years working out the details of one aspect of a first order problem, doing the work so splendidly and perfectly that you essentially 'nail it'. Or, you might want to forego perfection and depth in one narrow area and do smaller bits of work in a variety of different aspects of such first order problems. In that case, you may feel yourself to be a dilettante doing work in an opportunistic, superficial way. And, in a profound sense, you may be right.

There's probably no right answer to the foregoing question. Some guidance might be taken from S.S. Stevens, who would have recommended working on the first order problem (for sure), but working on a variety of aspects. Stevens' two favorite phrases were:

1. *As a first approximation.* Stevens would never say definitively that the value of 'so and so' (i.e., the exponent of the power function for sensory magnitude) was 'X'. Rather, at what seemed at first to be an affectation, Stevens would use the word *approximation.* However, that was the message. Despite years of experience and research, Stevens was instructing students that he and his colleagues were not measuring the precise value of the parameter, but just estimating it. And the lesson was, of course, deeper. Since Stevens was by then a 60+ year old Harvard professor, directing Harvard's Laboratory of Psychophysics, and not an amateur, this 'affectation' was teaching us that research *tries* to determine what's going on in the world, how the world works. The message was that the research was good, but not perfect. It wasn't worth being more perfect than the estimate. And, nature wouldn't let that happen anyway. There was always noise, the random variability of behavior, the monkey wrench that nature throws into our best laid plans.

2. *It's hard enough to know even the first significant digit.* In science, there's always a desire to probe deeper, to make measurements, to be precise. In Stevens' world, this precision was nonsense. One might measure precisely, but that didn't mean that one knew the precise value of a natural parameter. Stevens' work on perceived sensory magnitude (P) to physical intensity (I) generated an equation of the form $P = kI^n$. It was the exponent n that was of interest. According to

Stevens, despite all the effort that researchers might make, it would be sufficient to learn whether *n* was 0.3 or 0.4. More precision than that was fooling oneself.

What strategies of life work should you adopt?

If you have been reading this work in linear fashion, starting from the introduction and proceeding, then you'll realize that the message in this chapter is not a whole lot different from the messages in the other chapters. The entire book talks about the realities of a life of science, a life in science, the profession of research and research reporting. And, the book continues to come back to a basic theme; we're all human, fallible, of limited time on earth, and filled with a complex of needs, opportunities, abilities, and emotions.

But what about perfection today, about the research you're doing, about the path you're taking? Does the notion of good supplanting the perfect give you leave to do mediocre work? After all, if it's not perfect, then will almost anything do? If this sounds like some kind of sophistic argument, the type you might have as a college sophomore or first year grad student, it's not. Just because perfection is something to avoid spending too much time on does not give you permission to do a shoddy job, to cut corners, to escape the hard work of thinking and effort.

What should you do? Really, very simply, match your efforts to the problem. If you're young, don't get it into your head that your work is so important. Like your writing, it's not. You may wish on a star, on a hundred stars, on the grave of your great grandparents, or on the latest edition of some obscure scientific journal that you want to be great. Just aim for being good.

And, the practical advice here? Think about your problem, and think about what's enough to satisfy the really smart people in your field that it's a contribution. Think long and hard about what you're doing. And then do just enough to prove to yourself and to others that you have established a fact. Establish means that you convince others that you have discovered some aspect of nature. Don't belabor your discovery with 20 different ways of proving the validity of what you've discovered. Recognize that you're mortal, that undoubtedly, in the next ten years, people are either going to forget this fact, incorporate your findings into the general pool of knowledge, or disprove you. So, when you think about these three outcomes, do enough of the right research and writing to establish what you have found. And, don't overdo it.

1. When you can do a simple experiment, don't do a complicated, multi-factorial experiment with interactions. It just won't pay out. Of course, when you need interactions as part of your work, then by all means do so, but don't make the experiment overly complicated.

2. When you can establish the finding with 100 people, don't do 1,000 people just to get the extra precision. Precision is just that... how 'tight' your measurement is going to be. But, you're only human. Don't strive to be perfect. You're not G-d. And, the universe isn't going to come apart if you only have the first significant digit.

3. When you can establish the finding with a simple table and simple statistics, don't go for the fancy, esoteric analyses. Plotting data often tells a simpler story than regression modeling with all its statistics. In the end, people will judge with their own eyes and their own mind, not with SPSS®, Systat®, or SAS®. For you readers not familiar with these acronyms, they are the names of well-known, off-the-shelf statistical packages that can provide more statistics in 30 seconds that you may ever want to know.

If it can't be perfect, how much imperfection is allowable?

If it doesn't pay to do the perfect, then just how much imperfection should you accept? After all, when the work is too filled with errors, too rife with 'garbage', and simply too imperfect, it shouldn't be accepted. But then how do you know when 'enough is enough'? You cannot emotionally judge your own work. It's hard even for the most experienced researchers, the most polished writers, the most profound thinkers, to judge their own creations. The same thing holds with a family; it's not easy to really, objectively, judge your own children without emotion of some sort entering into the picture.

Every science has its own set of rules, norms for what is acceptable and what is not acceptable. Furthermore, '*not acceptable*' is, itself, a continuum. There is that level just below acceptable where a slight modification of the study in one small direction might make the difference. Then, there is the world of bias-filled research, which is hard to save unless one wants to do major surgery on the research and, even then, it's not certain whether one can achieve adequacy. And, finally, there is the world of work that, at least in one's opinion, is simply garbage, not salvageable, and not even worth thinking about. The hard thing to accept, especially when you are starting out in science, is that these three categories of sub-par work (below acceptable, biased, garbage) are not fixed categories, but vary by the science, by individual scientist, and by cultural norms of the day. That's why journals have several reviewers. What one person thinks is garbage another may swear is excellent.

How do you know what is acceptable and what is not and how should you plan your research accordingly? Instead of answering this question in the general sense, let's look at an example from the author's Ph.D. work in the psychophysics of taste. We can see some of the principles emerging from that work, which was done more than four decades ago in the Psychophysics Laboratory of Harvard University's Dept. of Psychology.

How psychophysics of taste taught 'adequacy' of research

By way of explanation, psychophysics is that chronologically oldest branch of experimental psychology which deals with the relation between physical stimuli and sensory responses. One of the major thrusts of psychophysics is to determine the exponent, n, of the power function relating sensory intensity (S) to physical intensity (I): $S = kI^n$.

In the 1960's, not a lot was known about the sense of taste and, of course, very little had been done to discover the value of the exponent, n. The experiment to discover 'n' is really quite simple, fortunately. One need only select the physical continuum (i.e., amount of sucrose), create a number of different concentrations (sugar + water mixtures), randomize these test stimuli, present them to the respondent, who in turn is instructed to assign a number to match the 'perceived sweetness'. This process is called magnitude estimation. It's a popular method for research. Magnitude estimates allow the respondent to be the 'measuring instrument' for sweetness (in the case of sugar + water at different concentrations).

For our purposes, the real question is how many respondents, i.e., study subjects, do we need in a single study to get 'good data'? That is, if we have 8 different concentrations of sucrose in water, how many ratings of each concentration should we gather before we feel comfortable that we have a good estimate of the exponent, n? This is a very practical question, pertaining to our notion of the 'perfect' versus the 'good'. When we have dozens or hundreds of ratings we will be more confident of our results, and have a better estimate of 'n'. On the other hand, it will take us a long time, and probably tax our patience. When we gather only 5-10 ratings we will be less confident of our results, because the data will be more variable and noisier. Yet we're less likely to tax our patience.

So what's the right answer, and why? Should we work ourselves to the bone for hundreds of ratings and 'nail' the exponent, or should we be satisfied with say 10-20 ratings for each stimulus, and come to our answer more quickly? This was a very practical problem, not so much because of one experiment with sugar, but because there were 80 different experiments of this type to run. For one experiment it's perfectly feasible to be obsessive. For 80 experiments it's not so feasible, especially when the objective of the research is to earn one's Ph.D.

The strategy was simple. It had become clear from previous studies conducted at the start of the research that about 20 ratings per test stimulus, and about 6-8 test stimuli of different concentrations sufficed to get a reasonable 'estimate' of the exponent 'n'. Of course one could reduce the number of judgments from 20 to say 12, and reduce the number of concentrations from 6-8 down to 4-5. However, from judgment it looked like it was possible to test one set of concentrations in a single day (6-8 levels of a test stimulus), especially if a single individual were to test each of the 6-8 levels, and do two 'rounds' or 'replicates'. With 10 individuals, it would be fair to conclude that one was getting a reasonable, if not superb, sample of judgments. But the truth of the matter was that one did not need to be any more accurate. The exponent 'n' emerged with 10 individuals, 2 replicates (20 judgments) and 8 concentrations. Thus each day could be one more experiment, from beginning to end.

The lesson here is that it wasn't necessary to be perfect. The goal of the Ph.D. exercise was to understand how the mind transformed the concentration of a solution of tastant materials solution into perceived sensory intensity (i.e., sucrose -→ perceived sweetness) and whether the presence of a masking agent (i.e., salt) changed the pattern. With 20 ratings per stimulus sample and with the appropriate set of 8 test stimuli one could generate reliable ratings. And, just as important, the thesis could proceed, step by step, with each day of 80 test days generating its set of data.

Summing up - Why do people try to do the 'perfect' when the 'good' is adequate?

It should become clear from the examples presented that one can go a long way in science without making the undue sacrifice of doing 'perfect' research. For most people, this type of thinking verges on the heretical. We are always taught to keep improving. Indeed, one of the sayings chanted by teens in summer camp is the well known ditty:

Good better best
Never let it rest
Until your good is better, and your better is best

This chapter goes against that popular wisdom. TIt presents an alternative; good enough, or in the words of Nobel Laureate Herbert Simon, 'satisficing'. It's not necessary to be perfect. Indeed, it may not even pay out. There may be a point beyond which the additional effort to go from good to very good, or from very good to excellent may be too costly, in time and in effort. If this doesn't seem reasonable, if it seems to compromise too much, just remember that a great deal of economics and business is done under conditions of constraints — deliver as much as possible, but within limits. The perfect may be wonderful, but just too hard, just too expensive. And, that goes for research efforts as well.

☆ ☆ ☆

PART 5

END NOTES

CHAPTER 24

MOVING ON

Part I – The Bad News

<u>Introduction</u>

In the 1970's, when I joined the commercial world after a stint at the U.S. Army Natick Laboratories as a senior scientist, I moved back to New York. At that time, the government had just started to recover from the oil shocks and the massive upward push which resulted from the Arab oil embargo of the early 1970's. It was not a propitious time to begin a new career.

Well, there was a lot to learn. The best place to learn the 'ropes', the sense of the business, was by seeing clients and, to a greater extent, going to conferences. These were not conferences filled with scientists presenting their latest discoveries, or cadres of young graduate students clucking over well known professors. Rather, these were a different kind of conference, trade conferences with talks, but also exhibitors and lots of 'stuff' (swag) to bring home. If one wanted to have a lifetime supply of combs, pencils, or key chains, here was the place, as long as the one wasn't particular about the fact that the swag had the company's name printed all over it.

The most important lessons from those conferences were the topics of the talks, which were about the practicalities of being in business. There was no pussyfooting around, political correctness where the topic was disguised in a socially acceptable manner. At least, that's what it seemed.

And so, some of the lessons about losing one's job first came out of those conferences. In fact, in those days there weren't many self-help books. You couldn't go to the nearest Barnes and Noble and be assaulted by a wall of self-help books, to gentle you through the times that you lost your job. But these conferences dealt with those issues.

<u>NOLF – No one lives forever</u>

One of the most important lessons I learned about losing one's job came from a presentation by Jeff Milam, former brand manager at a health and beauty aids company. Jeff's point in his very well attended presentation at the Cosmo Expo show in 1977 was NOLF – no one lives forever.

The key point of his presentation was that it's ok to lose one's job. It's not the worst thing in the world. It's not a measure of one's lack of worth. In fact, it's perfectly normal. In a world of creation and destruction, it's natural that a job will come, and go. It's natural for a person to occupy the job, while the job is vital, and then lose it.

The real key, according to Milam, is what you do with that opportunity while you have it. Jeff's point in 1977 still holds true a third of a century later. It is to 'what you will do' that we now turn.

What losing your job means for your next step

It's perfectly natural to lose your job. The real question is what do you do next? Of course, there are a lot of alternative paths. Some people feel that they need to sit down, relax, check out all of their 'options' and, of course, select the next opportunity which presents itself. Others, with the same qualifications, feel that the world has betrayed them, and that they must tell all of their friends. In this way, they release their feelings, getting rid of their anxiety. (And, if truth be known, boring everyone around them).

So what should you do? What is the best approach?

For this author, the best thing to do when he lost his job was to find another job. Or, to develop another job or a real business. That is, although it was tempting to take time off, to find out what one really and profoundly wanted to do, to discover oneself, the reality of the situation was that it was not the most productive route. We don't learn a lot by introspection. Most of us are better served by doing something than by thinking interminably about the slice of reality that we feel we rightfully occupy.

Oh, and one more thing. It's likely that everyone you meet, yes, virtually everyone, has at one time or other been rejected by his employer. This may not mean losing one's job, getting fired, or 'de-hired', or any of the other words that are used today, such as downsized, and so forth. It may be that the next person you meet is working at a lower salary, is a consultant, is between engagements, and so forth. The truth is that everyone's been there.

But how do you find another job?

As the economic downturn that began in 2009 continues to drag on, interminably, we see that stress sorts people out. It's worth looking at some of their reactions to unemployment, although I suspect that other authors can go into the topic with greater detail. Probably it's cathartic to them. Right now, however, let's see how different people react to losing a job:

1. <u>Deniers.</u> There are those who simply cannot believe that they and their beloved corporation are no longer joined at the hip. What is most fascinating

about these individuals is their Stockholm Syndrome. They identify with the organization that fired them. That is, they continue to think of the company as THEIR company, their employer. This unemployment thing, well that's just a momentary accident. Listening to them, you get a feeling that they believe the corporation did what had to be done, firing them. In fact, listening to them you come away with sadness and resignation; this is the way the world works. You do not get a sense that they come away with an active goal to find a new job. When we look at these people, we find very few researchers. In the main, the Deniers tend to be solid corporate types, middle management, who do not have many skills, have not been in many corporations, and really thought they would stay at the corporation for the rest of their lives. Researchers and scientists tend not to be Deniers. It may be that Deniers are so accustomed to the routines of the corporation that the corporation truly defines their world. In contrast, researchers and scientists have somewhat divided loyalties, between their field of specialization and their employer.

2. <u>Sad but clueless</u>. There is a whole group of individuals who are very sad that they lost their job, angry. Despite their feelings, and their intellectual knowledge of what happened, these individuals seem paralyzed and incapable of doing what has to be done. Many researchers and scientists are in this group. They realize that the world has changed, but they don't really know what to do.

3. <u>Networkers</u>. These individuals realize that their network may provide the opportunity for their next job. They aren't yet at the stage of reinventing themselves, but they do realize that the answer is through other people.

4. <u>Reinventers through entrepreneurship</u>. These individuals realize that they are alone, that the job isn't coming back, and that they must do something. Many of them reinvent themselves, becoming entrepreneurs. They decide to go into business for themselves. Some of them believe that they can offer corporate clients the same services as individuals that they did when they had jobs. Others realize that the companies need to buy 'products', not people, and proceed to reinvent themselves as 'products to be purchased'. That is, this second group do not sell themselves as people, but rather offer the company a 'productized service', with their time included.

<u>Summing up</u>

Losing your job is part of the game. It is likely that at some time in your career you will be de-hired, downsized, let go, or even downright fired. It's not so bad. Yes, it is a shock, and yes, it is rejection. It's not a figment of your imagination; you're out of a job.

On the other hand, it's not so bad. What you need is a good dollop of reality check-ing. It's probably not such a good idea to take six months off to 'find yourself'. When you look for yourself, you may be disappointed with what you discover.

It's a better idea to try to get back into the swing of things quickly. You can mourn the loss of your job. However, it's certainly better to create a new opportunity than it is to keep crying. We'll turn to a strategy of creating that opportunity in the next chap-ter. Meanwhile, when you lose your job, here's a hint; think about reinventing yourself and embedding yourself in a service-product that people can buy.

✦ ✦ ✦

Part II - You + vision + secret sauce

Introduction

In the world of employment, there are at least two species. There are those who want to take the corporate paycheck at regular intervals, to be sure that they have a job and, who, for the most part, are willing to put up with what the corporation deems to be necessary. Their jobs may be terrible, they may feel that their soul is sucked out on a regular basis, but the security of a paycheck is the ultimate 'pearl without price'. They are happy in the corporation, or at least not so miserable that they must leave.

We're not going to talk about them in this second section of the chapter. Their vision is happy attachment, and joyful dependency.

Instead, we will talk about those who realized that the road to personal happiness meant *not working for the corporation as an employee*. Nonetheless, they are tied to the corporation's money. One may not want to be an employee. However, people need to eat regularly, take vacations, educate their children, and enjoy the rewards of life.

Owning your job versus owning your business

When you work for another person or for a company, you exchange your time for a paycheck. When you have lost your job and are going to create a new life, you should ask yourself a simple question: *Do you want to rent your time or do you want to start a business?* We're not talking about working for a single company any more. Rather, we're talking about creating independence. Think about the two types of independence:

1. <u>Selling your own time</u>: Do you want to sell your time as a professional to different people? In this case, you are becoming a consultant. You are selling your time and your expertise. You may incorporate technology into your offerings, so that it's not pure time, but rather time+.

2. <u>Selling the time of others</u>: Or do you want to sell the services of people who work for you, or the use of technology that you develop? You may imbue people with your special expertise. However, and this is an important qualification; you have altered the nature of what you are doing. Now, you are selling something outside of yourself.

3. The easiest way to distinguish between choices #1 and #2 is to think about what would happen if you were to go on vacation for a year. Would you be as well

off, or almost as well off, when you returned? If the answer is NO, then you own your job. If the answer is YES, even a somewhat nervous YES, then you own your own business.

✳ ✳ ✳

OK – so what should a professional researcher do to own a business?

This book is about being a professional, not about starting a business. An entire world of business books awaits you. Since you're probably a professional or aspiring professional 'researcher', the question is 'how to start a business'.

Begin your quest by thinking about yourself as a product. That is, if it weren't you, but rather the knowledge and ability you have as a researcher, how could you package that so it doesn't require you?

This is a fairly tall order. Most people don't think of themselves as products, but rather as delivering a personal service. When people think of going into business, they think of themselves doing the work, of billing hours, much as a lawyer or a doctor bills for time, albeit in the form of both examination time and value-added 'tests'.

We're talking here of something different. The 'secret sauce' is not you yourself, but rather something that you can package, which can live outside of you.

Inventing your opportunity

Today's world runs on knowledge. Companies are evaluated, in part, on the degree to which they are able to innovate. Such innovation comes from knowing what the needs are, what the resources are, and how to reshape the resources to create new solutions, often hitherto undreamed of.

So, when you are a scientist, a researcher, what should you do to take advantage of the change in the world? After all, you are now living in what management guru Peter Drucker called the Knowledge Economy. You are knowledge workers. Now what should you do?

We'll end with a few suggestions and tips. These are not prescriptions of specifically what to do, but things you should think about. Let's start at the top:

1. Who you are and what you do: Your main focus is searching for patterns. Remember the discussion of psychophysics throughout this book. Psychophysics, that science which studies how our perceptions relate to the physical world, looks for patterns. This is the main thing you should keep in mind. You are in

the pattern discovery business. It's worth saying again. You are in the pattern discovery business.

2. <u>Other people have needs, agendas, predispositions</u>: People don't like to pay for other people. They like to pay for solutions. The focus of people is themselves, not you. So, even though you are in the pattern discovery business, no one else cares that business is about you. Now think about how patterns help them. Will patterns help them to make better products? Will patterns help them to communicate better messages? Think THEM, THEM, THEM. But, think THEM with what YOU have to offer. Sounds simplistic? It is, but I bet you didn't think of it before, though!

3. <u>Embedding YOU into something objective, outside you, often does the trick</u>: Think about packaging your ability to discover patterns into a computer-based technology. Can you embed your own knowledge into a computer program? The program need not be sophisticated and you can use it to support your own efforts. We have done this embedding twice.

    a. One of the tools, Product Engineer™, uses experimental design to lay out different combinations of formula variables. The optimizer then builds models, and identifies either the best formulation, or the formulation which fits a predefined pattern (reverse engineer). Notice that this technology embeds knowledge. So, with the technology we go automatically from selling oneself to selling projects, with the embedded technology. Yet that technology is simply one's own knowledge, in a formalized computer program.

    b. The second tool is IdeaMap®.net (www.IdeaMap.net), a do it yourself technology, which allows the user to mix and match ideas, test them among consumers, and get the answers in automated format, within 12 hours. It also has a version for package design. The key is that the program embeds a different type of knowledge, also using experimental design. And, by means of the technology, it becomes possible to create a business, in which one's own knowledge is the driving force, but not the workhorse. That is, with IdeaMap®.net, one can create a business, not simply own a job.

<u>Summing up</u>

As a professional, YOU are the secret sauce. But, as a professional, a scientist who is regrouping, starting anew, it's incumbent upon you to change your way of thinking about yourself. Right now, you own your job. The goal is to create a business. The business comes from YOU, yourself.

And, the essence of the business, its secret sauce? Fundamentally, capitalize on what you're best at. In general, you are probably best at spotting and using patterns. That's what scientific training is all about; not technician work, but science work.

You also have to realize that people buy solutions and not other people. The world isn't waiting for you to arrive at their doorstep, with YOURSELF. Maybe your mother is, but that's about it. Sell the project, solve the problem using technology, and make sure parts of YOU are embedded in the technology.

The rest is specifics. And, of course, the devil is in the details. By the way, when you keep at it, at some point you'll overcome the hurdles. Success is just over the horizon. Don't ever give up. Happy hunting!

✧ ✧ ✧

CHAPTER 25

REFLECTIONS ON BECOMING A FOSSIL
IN A SEDIMENTARY LAYER

Introduction

Now, we are coming to the end of our visit together. When I began this book, I originally conceived of the topics and issues in what one might loosely call the professional's life. These topics would range from one's earlier education in college to one's early middle years on the job, whether it be in a laboratory 'pumping out the stuff of science', or in a company.

What came out instead was a wonderful surprise, at least to me, the writer. The surprise was that it was the 'me', the 'I', Miss Piggy's 'moi' that kept intruding. As I kept pushing the 'me' away in favor of science, fact, and third-part prescription of 'thou shalt do' or 'you oughta try this', the self kept intruding back. The little person in the back of my head kept demanding that the writing focus, not so much on what one should do, as what 'I' did, and why.

And so, you have an intensely personal book here. Yes, there are observations about the world in which you or, more realistically, I live. There aren't too many guide books to this wonderful land of professionalism which deal with the specifics, the daily arm wrestles, and pleasures and some of the pain. At least, there aren't too many guide books from someone who has been there, and who is writing from a combination of self-help and autobiography.

But what are the lessons?

Lessons, specific ones, comprise a continuing topic in this book, an ongoing theme or *leitmotif* as the musicians like to say. If you have any sense of history, you know that the most interesting history 'reads' are those where the author tries to look for patterns, for motives, for something beyond the old line 'one damned thing after another'. And so that theme of patterns, of reasons, of lessons, is an essence of this book. The important thing is the lessons, the learning, the wisdom of a professional life. Or, to use another oft-quoted line, this time from the movies, '*What's it all about Alfie?*'

If we were to summarize the key lessons of this book, we might come away with the following ten. So, here they are:

1. The odds are that you're going to live a long time. Don't mess up the feeding trough that will be the source of your professional growth and, more than likely, your livelihood. Be sensitive about what you do. Things do come back to bite. You don't want that to happen. Period.

2. Kindness, kindness, kindness. I once read an blog which stated that *'when I was young I admired cleverness; now that I'm old I admire* kindness'. You can't be too kind. It will pay dividends. Don't worry about wasting kindness. Just be kind.

3. What you do as a young professional is excusable. You may think that an error you make when you are young will follow you around. Chances are that no one notices it, or if someone notices it when you are young, it will be forgotten.

4. The pen is mightier than the sword. It helps to practice writing. When you write to be read (not to be remembered, to be read), you may be pleasantly surprised. Think of your writing as an investment that you make and forget. Sometimes, unexpected dividends show up in the mail. That's good.

5. Publish a lot. When you start out no one cares, even if you have ground-breaking work. Your goal is to get beyond the beginning stage, to create a corpus of your own work. That work will support you; I promise.

6. Everyone gets rejected from journals. It's not worth killing yourself over. The peer review system is flawed, but so what? If you don't get it published in an 'A' journal, try a 'B' journal, and then a 'C' journal. Just get it published.

7. When you look for something to be right, it's better to be 80% right and on time than 100% right and late. When you miss the train, miss the boat, miss the chance, it's gone. Do not let the perfect be the enemy of the good.

8. If you're miserable in your job, your post-doc or whatever, remember that you can generally move. If worst comes to worst, and it does, think about going out as a consultant. You can then get fired by each client and still survive. What a wonderful lesson. Change, don't die.

9. You're not as important as you think you are. Abandon your *amour propre*. You're not that important at all. So enjoy life. By the time you become very important, you'll either be old or dead and you won't be able to enjoy life very much. Arthritis happens; that's the least of it. *Carpe diem*; seize the day.

10. Educate yourself so that you understand more than a simple, narrow field. It helps to read history, literature and philosophy. It's even interesting. There was a world before you were born, there were ideas before you were weaned. The truth is, these will be there long after you're gone. So imbibe some culture; and not just the culture in yogurt. You'll be a better scientist and professional because of it.

✿ ✿ ✿

Tam Venishlam
Shevach le K' Boreh Olam

In grateful, loving memory of my parents

Moses Moskowitz
Moshe b Admor Yisroel Elimelech and Miriam

Leah Moskowitz
Leah b R' Tzvi and Tamar

May their memories remain a blessing

✿ ✿ ✿